REAL
CLOTHES

Real

Real clothes are practical, long-lasting, and have enduring beauty. Because they're designed to satisfy a specific occupational requirement—not the whims of fashion—they never go out of style. And because most are manufactured with quantity purchase in mind, they're eminently affordable.

Dedicated to Mao Zedong

CLOTHES

By J. C. Suarès and Susan Osborn
Photographs by Don Hamerman
Introduction by Caterine Milinaire
Designed by Traci Churchill
Compiled by Kevin Osborn
Index of Sources Edited by Caroline Spangenberg

Quill
New York 1984

Text copyright © 1984 by Susan Osborn
Design copyright © 1984 by J. C. Suarès
Photos copyright © 1984 by Don Hamerman
Introduction copyright © 1984 by Caterine Milinaire

All rights reserved. No part of this book may be reproduced or utilized in any form or by any means, electronic or mechanical, including photocopying, recording or by any information storage and retrieval system, without permission in writing from the Publisher. Inquiries should be addressed to William Morrow and Company, Inc., 105 Madison Avenue, New York, N.Y. 10016.

Library of Congress Catalog Card Number: 83-61794

ISBN: 0-688-02158-1
ISBN: 0-688-02159-X(pbk)

Printed in the United States of America

First Quill Edition

1 2 3 4 5 6 7 8 9 10

Don't fight 'em, join 'em, on page 88.

On our cover: model Julie Barth in a grease-monkey suit. Photograph by Jack Deutsch. Cover styled by Deborah Baker.

To the best of the authors' and the publisher's knowledge the information contained herein was accurate as of the date of printing. They also disclaim all responsibility for the merchandise. Any inquiries should be directed to the appropriate catalog house.

PHOTO CREDITS

Page 2 *Sovfoto*
Page 4 *China Photo Service, Bejing, China*
Page 5 *Norman Rockwell*
Pages 7, 14, 18, 46, 47, 52, 68, 72, 86, 122, 123, 134 bottom, 137, 160 *New York Public Library Picture Collection*
Page 11 *NASA*
Page 15, 67, 69 *Wideworld*
Pages 21, 21, 26, 27 *Courtesy Danskin Inc.*
Pages 31, 36, 91 *Library of Congress*
Pages 34-35, 144 *Smithsonian Institution*
Pages 92-93 *Firefighting Museum, New York City*
Page 110 *American Red Cross*
Pages 111, 121 *National Archives*

Contents

Behind The Scenes
leggings • leotards • rip-stop overalls • slippers

12

Maximum Function
aprons • crossover jackets • slush boots • clogs

28

The Great Outdoors
ski jumpsuits • hunting shoes • explorers' bags • jodhpurs • jockey silks

44

Sportschic
hockey jerseys • cyclists' gloves • warm-up suits • baseball jackets • boxers' robes

64

Action-Tested Fashion
rainwear • suspenders • attack coats • boots

88

Medical Magic
scrub suits • smocks • capes • nurses' shoes

106

Uncle Sam
guernseys • helmets • combat boots • document pouches

118

Cowboy Elegance
jeans • spurs • chaps • boots • overalls

132

....

The Best Real Clothes Catalogs

145

Norman Rockwell's Boy Scout takes the Real Clothes oath. For the official Boy Scout Catalog, see the Index.

"Quality is what it's about," says writer and real clothes afficionado, Caterine Milinaire, seen here.

Maureen Lambray

Introduction
by Caterine Milinaire

"Excuse me, but where did you get this great outfit you are wearing?" is a question I have found myself asking complete strangers on the street and often being asked. Is it a flattering question in order to engage conversation with someone seemingly interesting? Rarely. Most of the time it has to do with that long quest people engage in: finding something to wear that works. Ever since daily activities have gone beyond the hunter-gatherer-cave-people stage, animal skins and furs have become impractical (a little cumbersome for dancing at a celebration or to lay bricks). The working clothes of today are made of the best cloths and threads and are designed to be functional and last a long time. They are the "real clothes" that this book is about.

Fashion trends have always fascinated me. In "Cheap Chic," a book I co-authored in 1975, there was a great emphasis on finding personal style in functional clothes. "Cheap Chic" to me, meant how to pull yourself

Time was, cowboys, and cowgirls, too, hated denim—the first person to buy a pair of Mr. Levi Strauss' denim pants was a gold miner. But by the end of the 19th century if you rode the range you wore blue jeans. Except, of course, if the social custom kept you in skirts.

All-cotton Kung Fu uniform isn't just for fighting. These heavyweight jackets have plenty of pockets, and roll-back sleeves with crisp white lining.

Glare-cutting side flaps have made these mountaineering glasses popular with those of us whose only climbing may be a flight of stairs.

together on not much money yet make an aesthetic (and political) statement. Aesthetic, because I enjoy beautifying this planet with combinations of colors and textures, infusing a little humor and whimsy along the corporate concrete maze. Political, in the sense that whether or not one has money it is presumptuous to show one's financial status through clothes. Overdressing often intimidates and renders communication with others more difficult. I know for a fact that when I travelled in China recently I could not have mingled so unobtrusively in the back streets of Kunming had I not worn Mao blues.

When I first came to America from France over a decade ago, people often commented on what I wore as being eccentric amalgam. I knew however that the dance leotard, the many pocketed chinese jacket, the sailor's pants and the tennis shoes I wore then made some sense. It was only a matter of time until active clothes gained popularity.

Looking back on it I see I was only acting in the true pioneer spirit of the settlers. Prairie folks out west had no shops to indulge their vestimentary needs. It was through mail-order catalogs on a minimum budget that they purchased their workshirts, overalls and cowboy boots. Could it be that the pleasure of doing shopping at home, for tried and true quality items, has come full circle in this busy world of hard working people?

Mao Now! Magazine designer Wanda Yueh's updated paean to the great Chinese uniform is by French designer Michel Klein. The Mao jacket makes sense for millions—anything this comfortable should.

Because quality is what it's about when one orders from professional sources. The fabric has to be sturdy for a baker's apron to withstand endless laundering. The cut of an intern's shirt must give maximum ease to be functional and French Foreign Legion boots are made of top canvas and rubber to withstand twenty mile hikes. The old mail-order houses are still around because they deal in these perennial factors: classic shapes and quality.

It may well be that "L'habit ne fait pas le moine" (or roughly translated from the French saying: "Clothes do not make the man") but wearing a fisherman's bright yellow slicker when lost out at sea in a storm will help you being seen from afar and staying dry. By not being soaked to the bone you can catch the fish you need to survive. If you are lucky you will be found at which point you can tell the rescue party that the slicker does not make the fisherman.

Real clothes: the next phase.

International restaurateur Roger Choukroun owns at least a dozen pairs of the exact same Christian Dior shoes, but when he wants to deal strongly with a task at hand, he slips on his wrestling shoes, of which he only needs two pairs.

Stretch out in professional dancewear by Danskin and Capezio. Cotton and spandex leotard over cotton tights, paired with leg warmers. You'll feel more fit just putting these clothes on! Model: Jacqueline Schementi of Kay Models.

I

BEHIND THE SCENES

leggings • leotards • rip-stop overalls • slippers

Working clothes donned by dancers, painters, and sculptors are often as creative and idiosyncratic as their work. One might choose to work as Rembrandt sometimes did, swathed in oversized velvet and mink robes; another might prefer to work as Isadora Duncan did, nearly in the nude. Whatever the individual style, you can be sure that all artists' working clothes do one thing and one thing well: They ensure maximum freedom of movement. Nothing is permitted that might inhibit or in any way constrain the muse.

DANCERS

A direct descendant of court entertainments, ballet was originally a costly entertainment performed solely for the long-nosed and ennui-suffering members of the sixteenth-century Italian aristocracy. Those who performed in these distractions (alternately known as mummings, masquerades, and interludes) were forced to practice in their everyday clothes: Bewigged men garbed in stiff coats and knee-breeches struggled to keep their swords from interfering with their *pliés*, while women confined in tight-laced, long-sleeved bodices and panniered skirts gasped for breath as they were tossed between the devil and the knight. Onstage, performers were dressed similarly; costumes of the time were a profusion of tiers and

Dancers with the Paris Opera Ballet, in 1929.

Real Clothes 15

In this photograph from the 1900's, dance pupils surround their mentor, the great dancer Isadora Duncan. Instead of the confining dancewear then in vogue, Duncan believed that a dancer's clothing should be loose and unrestricting.

Editorial assistant Benita Ricks in a supremely comfortable dance-inspired tank jumpsuit by Transit, for Charivari. A flowing headband and a fabric belt add soft dimension to the outfit.

flounces. In some ballets, costumes were overtly and ludicrously symbolic: A troubador, for example, might be dressed in contemporary street clothes, but he would be ornamented from top to toe with sheet music, violas, bows, and recorders. Similarly, an architect might be decorated with a Corinthian cap (worn as a hat), pilasters, friezes, squares, and rules.

During the first years of ballet, women were rarely permitted to perform (most female roles were played by men), but during the seventeenth century, when ballet moved across the continent to England and France, women began executing leaps and turns as difficult as those performed by their male counterparts. As is easily imagined, their whirling skirts, no matter how stiff, raised not just a few eyebrows and necessitated the invention of a protective garment known as *calecon de précaution* or, literally translated, "precautionary drawers." Once designed to ensure modesty, these drawers, or tights as we know them today, are now occasionally worn skirtless.

The French Revolution fomented dramatic changes in almost every areas of life, including the life in the theater. For the first time, people off and on the streets dressed unashamedly, in fact almost defiantly, in "work clothes." While ballet directors were reluctant to part with the opulent display onstage, behind the curtain, choreographers and teachers ordered their protégés to discard their cumbersome clothing in favor of lighter attire that would better reveal technical faults and anatomical defects. By the middle of the nineteenth century, choreographers all over Europe were singing the praises of that marvelous innovation designed by the original man on the flying trapeze, Jules Léotard.

Born in 1838, Léotard, with his incomparable physique and curly black hair (as well as a natural inclination for the dramatic), was the archetypal nineteenth-century showman. Because he preferred "a natural garb which does not hide your best features," Léotard wore a skintight maillot while performing his daring aerial stunts. In defense of modest eyes, Léotard did, however, wear an abbreviated fringed skirt over his body sheath.

With the development of stretch nylon in the 1950s, this body-hugging garment became one of the most comfortable and affordable pieces of clothing available. And what could be more convenient for a dancer moving from town to town—or a student, a stewardess, a photographer, or a model—than a comfortable, snap-crotch bodysuit that rolls up into a ball, needs no ironing, and can be washed out in the sink?

Onstage, classical ballet costumes have not changed much since the nineteenth century. Other than the diminution of the ballerina's skirt (necessitated by the development of nearly acrobatic tours de force), the classical costume remains much as it was in 1832 when M. Taglioni danced the lead role in the first performance of *La*

Sylphide. La Sylphide was the first ballet to evince a Romantic influence; during Taglioni's performance, she wore an inverted corolla of white gauze complemented by tiny wings at the shoulders and a garland of convolvuli in her hair. To complete the effect, a posy pinned to her breast rose and fell with well-timed if delicate gasps. This gossamer costume enveloped Taglioni in a milky haze and rendered her ethereal and phantomlike, more imaginary than real.

So enraptured were choreographers with Taglioni's frail delicacy that they began demanding the etherealization of all their performers. Thus dancers were, for the first time, required to stand on their toes. Unfortunate thing was, nobody had, at the time, thought of pointe shoes. In an attempt to cushion their toes, Taglioni and others darned the tips of their eminently pliable slippers with heavy thread, but it was only after the recurrence of strained muscles and bleeding digits that a humane choreographer suggested blocking the toes. Even though the tips of contemporary dancing shoes are hard enough to take the weight off the bunion joint (hard enough, many novitiates lament, to make an embarrassing thud if their *pas de bourrées* are not controlled), many continue to darn the toe as the woven thread helps grip the floor securely.

When Isadora Duncan appeared onstage in 1904, she dealt the traditional ballet costume the severest blow it had received since the French Revolution. Duncan berated the traditional costume and its advocates: One does not play piano with gloved hands, one should not dance with one's body similarly sheathed. For Duncan, the most important criterion was that the costume leave the dancers' arms and legs unencumbered; through her efforts, modern dancers were liberated from their confining skirts, tight bodices, restricting tights, and uncomfortable shoes.

Duncan did not, however, find anything unacceptable about leggings, these wool and now orlon and acrylic overgarments used by dancers throughout the twentieth century to keep their leg

Andrew Thomas, a student at the prestigious School of American Ballet, wears their traditional practice uniform—a simple white tee, black Capezio tights and ballet slippers.

Capezio's catalog of dance and exercise clothing is highlighted by exciting glimpses backstage in the dance world.

The German painter Caspar David Friedrich in his studio, by Friedrich George Kersting, 1811.

Artist Nina Duran in her New York studio. "I often work in a jumpsuit because they're so—well—comfortable, and I always wear this apron which I transplanted from the kitchen."

muscles warm while practicing or waiting. Though most of us who wear them for comfort and convenience buy them ready-made, many dancers still knit their own while waiting backstage or for the flight to the next performance.

If you're in the market for comfortable and easy-to-care-for casual wear, don't limit yourself to leotards and leggings. When taken out of the practice room, Capezio's orlon knit camisole top "solotard" with elastic stirrups makes one of the sexiest pieces of loungewear around. Or try Danskin's lightweight rip-stop nylon overalls. This handsomely designed cover-up comes with a removable elasticized belt and has a camisole bodice and elasticized ankles to facilitate free and easy movement. While pointe shoes may not be the best for around the house, "Canadian" dance slippers are. Available in twelve colors, these featherweight slippers have stretch nylon uppers and leather soles and they're guaranteed to last for years.

PAINTERS AND SCULPTORS

Researching the evolution of artists' working clothes is a difficult task. One can turn to self-portraits, but one must bear in mind that the artist would most likely have painted the image the way he or she would like to appear. When Matisse, for example, was photographed painting a model dressed in a rather splendid state of Turkish *déshabillé*, he wore a conservative tweed suit, a white shirt, and a polka-dot tie. Braque, on the other hand, often presented himself in a casual smock coat. Rembrandt, as we've seen, liked to envelop himself in mink and ermine, and Courbet was a man for stripes: When he dressed for his part in his painting *Das Atelier des Malers*, he wore a gray coat with black-and-gray striped lapels, buttons, and cuffs that matched (or mismatched, depending on your particular sensibility) his moss green and brown horizontally striped trousers.

Legend has it that it was Augustus John who, after a romantic if brief sojourn to Paris, was the first academic painter to don a smock, a full tie, and an oversized beret. This flamboyant style was quickly adopted by "Sunday painters" of the nineteenth century who stood on the banks of the Thames and the Seine in full regalia, often sporting a lackey to wipe untidy dribbles from the tips of their brushes.

In general, it seems safe to say that an artist, be he or she Picasso or Nevelson, will wear whatever is comfortable and non-restricting. Philip Pearlstein, for example, wears flannel shirts, blue jeans, and Chinese cloth slippers: "They are light and the plastic soles help keep the floor clean—foam soles put down dirt." Because his work clothes are simple and inexpensive, they can be replaced easily when they become so hardened with a similar outfit: blue jeans (many times mended by his wife) and an old cotton shirt.

Above, Danskin's Unitards. Sleek slim lines on stage or off—these unitards come long sleeved, short sleeved, or as a scoop neck tank top. They're made of 85% nylon, 15% Lycra spandex, and you can use them for dance, exercise, or even as insulators for winter sports.

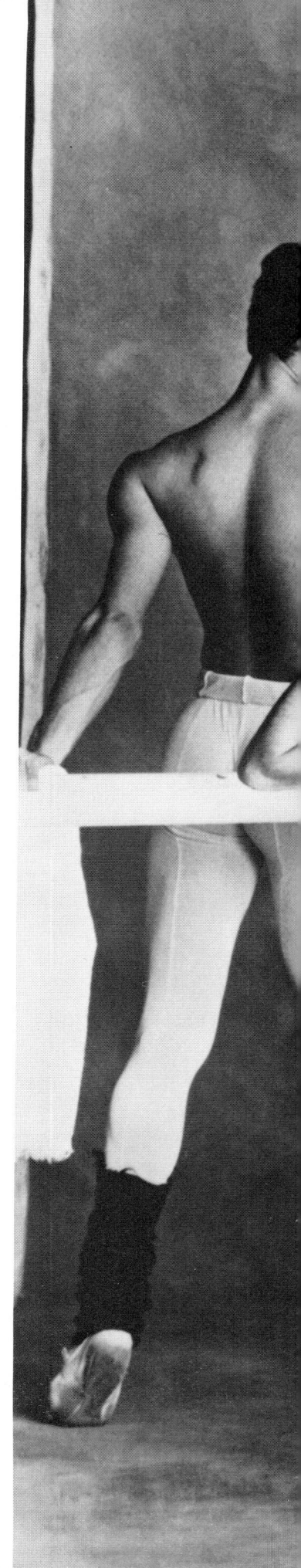

Right, also by Danskin, leotards in every conceivable color, fabric, and style—scoop neck, v-fronts, turtlenecks, camisoles, long sleeve, short sleeve . . . you get the idea. To get the clothes, you can find Danskin products through mail order catalogs like Taffy's (see Index).

Legwarmers from Capezio's brand-new dance/exercise line of bodywear. They're made of 100% acrylic-knit yarn and are shown here in Dusty Rose (right) and Black. Dancers wear them to keep their leg muscles warm, but you can try them layered over tights or even jeans to add certain bounce to your everyday gait.

A *cast of thousands, or so it seems—stirrup tights, seamless tights, tights without feet, fishnet tights—if that's not enough, they come in about thirty different colors. By Capezio. They've been dancing since 1887.*

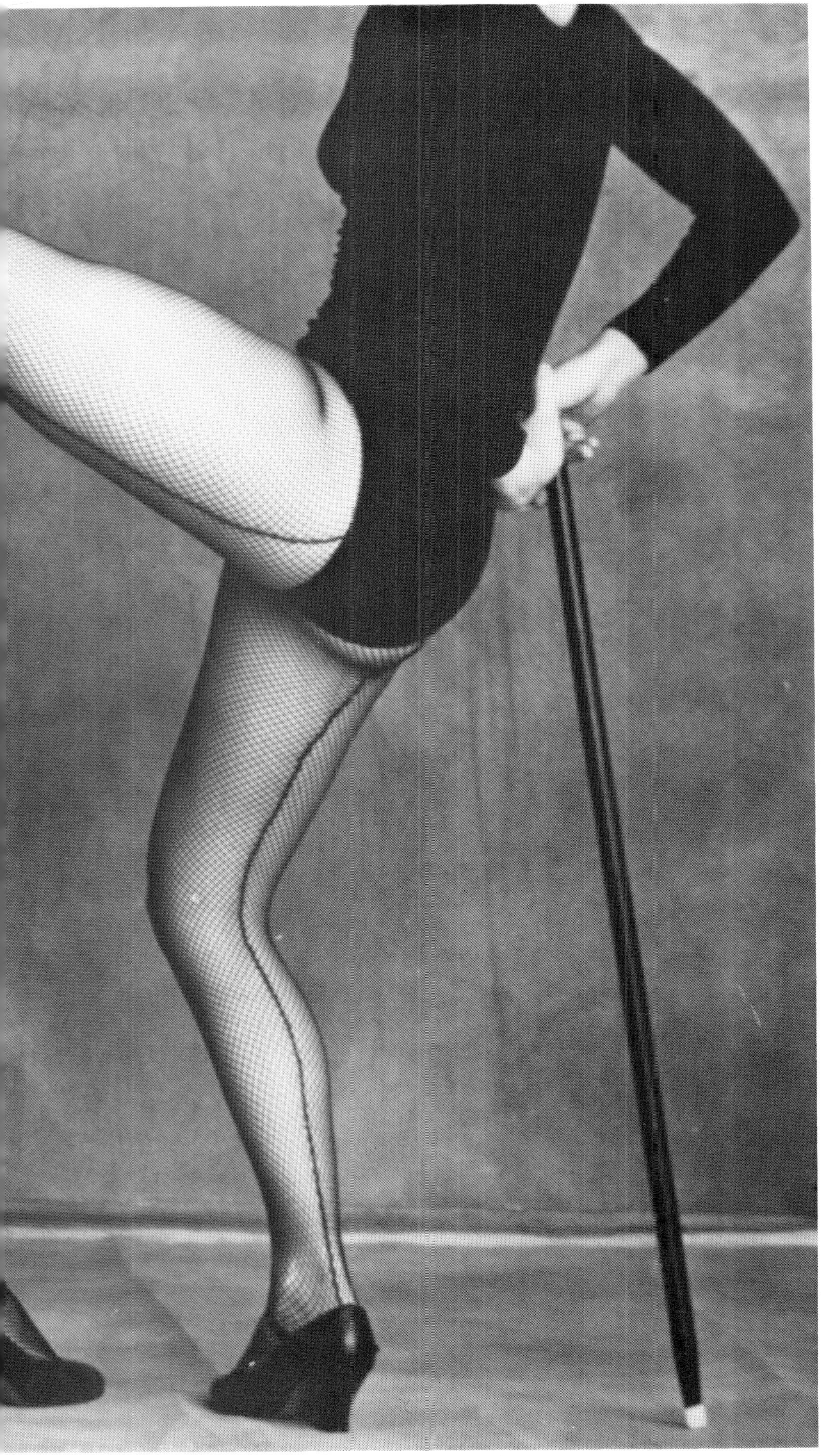

Fishnet tights! The pair in the middle even have sewn-in nylon feet for extra comfort. By Danskin, but we think they look great off stage too.

You probably didn't know that the original man on the flying trapeze, Jules Leotard, invented the garment which now carries his name. Below, our model takes it from the trapeze to the tennis court.

2

MAXIMUM FUNCTION

*aprons • crossover jackets •
slush boots • clogs*

Incredible style and all-cotton comfort! Model Ann Marie Forget bounding by in a white cotton house dress and vibrant red and white smock often worn by pizza chefs and food vendors. Clothing courtesy O.K. Uniform, New York City.

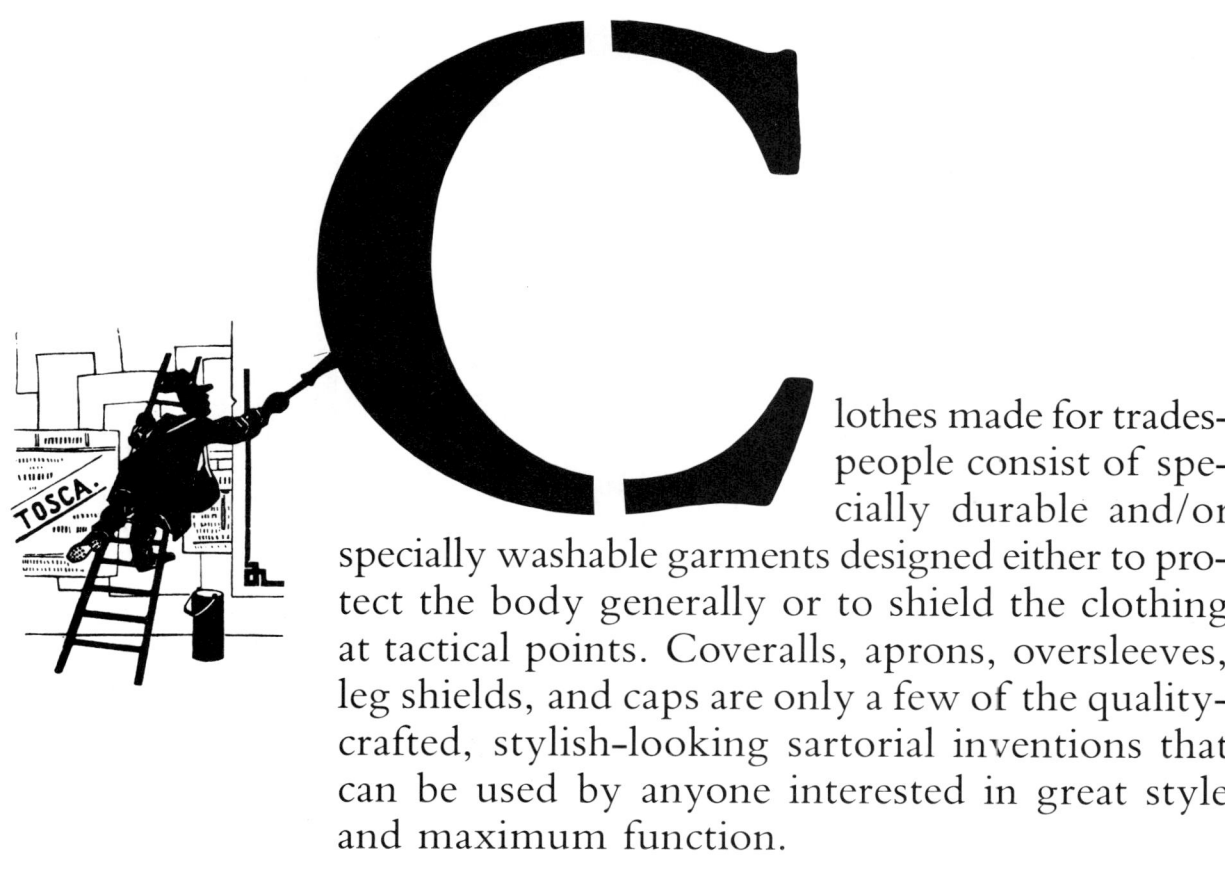

C

lothes made for tradespeople consist of specially durable and/or specially washable garments designed either to protect the body generally or to shield the clothing at tactical points. Coveralls, aprons, oversleeves, leg shields, and caps are only a few of the quality-crafted, stylish-looking sartorial inventions that can be used by anyone interested in great style and maximum function.

CARPENTERS, BUILDERS, SMITHS

It was not until the nineteenth century, when carpenters began sporting paper caps, that any kind of garment distinguished them from their fellow workers. During the first half of the 1800s, when paper became inexpensive (as late as 1818, it had been a punishable offense in England to produce a newspaper exceeding twenty-two by thirty-two inches), carpenters folded a small square hat to protect their hair, keep it out of their eyes, and mark them as members of a particular occupation. Descendents of this cap are still worn by workers on building sites in Rome, by house painters, and by bakers and others who work in trades where a high standard of hygiene is required.

The most important sartorial innovation discovered by carpenters and other members of the building trades in the fifteenth century was the apron. This simple and unpretentious garment was

M*en at work wearing the basics—right up to the paper bag hats.*

During World War II, when all of "our boys" were fighting overseas, women filled the ranks in factories here at home. Of course they quickly understood which working clothes made the grade, so thousands of "Rosie the Riveters" jumped into jumpsuits.

Joan Marino whips up tonight's special edition while wearing a newspaper vendor's apron. They always have deep, roomy pockets and can take almost anything you can dish out!

first made of leather and was designed to protect builders, tinkers, and joiners from wayward slivers of wood and metal. At first, aprons were made of a whole skin, thus permitting one of the five corners to be used as a bib and attached to the coat or waistcoat button by a buttonhole. If the skin was square, the apron would be attached by a loop at the back of the neck.

This unassuming article was quickly designated an imperative accessory and served satisfactorily to protect metalsmiths and coopers from sparks and friction, shoemakers and cobblers from rubbing and wax, and tanners and slaughterhouse workers from splashes and knife injuries.

Throughout the centuries, tradespeople have made aprons of any sturdy material that would best suit their purposes. The first cloth aprons, for example, were made of durable woolens like stammel or serge—early serge was so coarse, workers could use it to abrade the dirt from their hands. By the nineteenth century, fishermen found that oilskin made the best apron for their purposes, while woodcutters fashioned aprons of hemp. Today, heavy rubber aprons are manufactured for use by people working in fish and meat markets and in chemical works.

Ever since Noah got started on his ark, tradespeople have looked for comfortable work boots that are water- and mud-resistant and sturdy enough to protect tender toes from falling hammers and pieces of metal. Mind you, this has been no easy task: Like well-diggers, who worked mainly in the buff, leech collectors of the early nineteenth century gave up the fight and wore no shoes at all. A primitive kind of work boot, however, was developed as early as the fourteenth century. This flap-front boot fastened at the side and is almost identical in conception, if not construction, to the boots many welders wear today. The now ubiquitous clog was another early work shoe. Because the wooden sole is water-resistant and prevents the conduction of heat, field workers in Scandinavia found it to be the ideal shoe for working in damp yards.

BUTCHERS

Like their counterparts in other trades, butchers of the Middle Ages wore short tunics, perhaps some kind of simple headgear, sandallike shoes, and absolutely no protective garments whatsoever. But by the seventeenth century they, as had their fellows, recognized that even a modest apron could increase longevity. Thus this unsung device became, once again, the essential accessory.

The first aprons of choice, rather tellingly called "fleshers," were made of cotton or wool. Later, butchers found that aprons of jean, drill, and century cloth best suited their purposes. By the nineteenth century, slaughterhouse workers wore aprons of black or yellow oilskin.

A *lot has changed since Norman Strum, M.D. (that's Meat Dealer) first became a butcher 33 years ago—but not the style of his apron. Butcher's aprons are always longer than those worn by other tradespeople—the extra length serves to keep their pants clean when handling large sides of beef.*

It's been a long time now since you could get the finest food and service while whizzing across America on the Chicago Limited.

E*ver since ice cream was a nickel, you could trust the man in white.*

Butchers were one of the first group of laborers to recognize the benefits of oversleeves. These cloth or occasionally leather sheaths covered a butcher's coat sleeve from waist to elbow and protected it from splashes. Although these prophylactic garments were troublesome to keep up before the invention of elastic in the 1820s, they were a satisfactory shield against at least one of the many hazards of the job. Leather oversleeves are still used by tradespeople today, including welders, who use them to protect their forearms against molten metal.

Given the nature of the job, butchers also found leg shields a handy accessory. These shin guards resembled hockey pads and helped keep a butcher's trousers relatively respectable-looking.

Leg protectors did not, however, originate with nineteenth century butchers. Leg shields have been worn since the Middle Ages by a variety of tradespeople to help protect them from pressure, sparks, and splashes. The first "bams" or "gamashes" (as leggings were known until the nineteenth century) worn by field workers to protect them from inadvertent scythe slices were primitive wraparounds, made of any thick, coarse stuff available. Gradually leggings were made with buckles or buttons at the side, and by the nineteenth century printers wore full-length leg shields attached at the top to an apron.

MILLERS, BAKERS, COOKS

Because millers, bakers, and cooks are liable to be covered with flour, they have always worn white, and it is this whiteness that distinguishes them from all other tradespeople.

The often oppressive heat in kitchens and mills has made cooks and other kitchen workers loath to wear any kind of overgarment, protective or otherwise. At some time two or three hundred years ago, they did however adopt the white cap that we still expect to see when a chef emerges from the kitchen to receive his or her kudos.

According to most sources, bakers acquired their caps sometime between 1664 and 1731, and they have, since then, been worn in a variety of shapes and sizes. Most seem to have settled on the tam-o'-shanter style now favored by French *pâtissiers*, for it was this flat-topped cap that most facilitated carrying trays laden with pastries on the head.

Cooks have also donned caps. The *toque*, the stiff white cap we are most familiar with, came into fashion early in the nineteenth century. Although some preferred the tam-o'-shanter style favored by bakers and others the skullcap or "porkpie" style with the tassel, it is the "cauliflower" style that seems most popular with chefs today.

Cooks have also traditionally worn neckcloths to absorb perspiration: If the chef was asked to make an appearance before a group of satisfied guests, this handy accoutrement could double as a cravat.

During the nineteenth century, the preferred jacket was a crossover French-style coat designed not to gap. The slit-wrist cuffs can be easily rolled back, making this jacket a handy complement for both professional and amateur chefs.

Clothes designed for contemporary tradespeople are made to be especially comfortable, durable, and easy to care for. They're also one of the best fashion bargains around. Lightweight coveralls, for example, designed with tapered legs, elastic side inserts, and two-way zippers, can be purchased for under $25. Long-tailed, fully cut workshirts made of wrinkle-free blends and reinforced on all points of strain, are also inexpensive. Sexy speedsuits, worn by auto racers and mechanics, are formfitting and breatheable, and the pleated back and elastic waist inserts ensure extra comfort. Rubber, leather, and denim work aprons are fully cut, practical, and made with plenty of deep pockets. Or try a pair of slush boots: These fully lined boots pull over your shoes, fasten with adjustable strap buckles, and have safety-ensuring knurled rubber soles.

38 Real Clothes

Bakers originally wore white to camouflage the mounds of flour they inevitably spilled upon themselves while working, but model Doug Atelean thinks that this 100% cotton baker's shirt looks great outside the kitchen too. Courtesy OK Uniform.

Real Clothes 39

Unbelievable! This jumpsuit, made from an impermeable "miracle fabric" is actually disposable! Belted, worn over a colorful tee, and sportily rolled at the cuffs, model Tara Engler's paper jumpsuit is ready to go anywhere. Jumpsuit courtesy Melco (see Index). Makeup by Debra Lehman.

Real Clothes 41

Magson Uniform's heavy-duty work-wear can be dressed up or down. Our opening spread features an all-cotton work dress similar to those shown here, but belted and accessorized for a completely different look. Or be on your guard with genuine "security" clothing like the hat, jacket, and pants shown here.

Angelica's catalog is at your service—genuine waiter's and bartender's wear are just some of the things featured.

Coveralls, smocks, and workshirts can all be pressed into service as sturdy additions to your everyday wardrobe. All items on these two pages are available from *Magson Uniforms*, and they come in a surprising array of colors—try a jumpsuit, for instance, in red, orange, navy, green, white, gray, or postman blue.

3

THE GREAT OUTDOORS

ski jumpsuits • *hunting shoes* • *explorers' bags* • *jockey silks* •

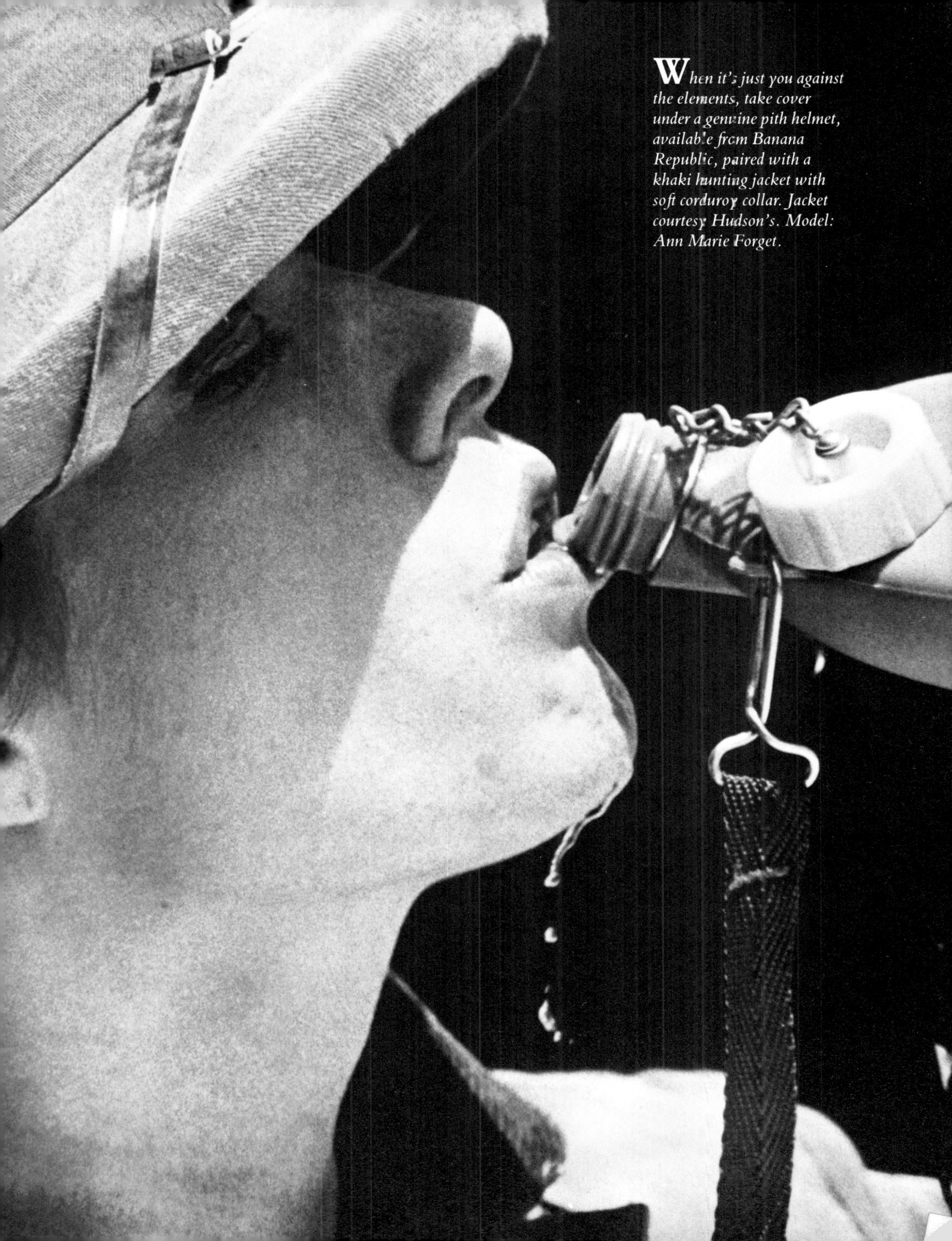

When it's just you against the elements, take cover under a genuine pith helmet, available from Banana Republic, paired with a khaki hunting jacket with soft corduroy collar. Jacket courtesy Hudson's. Model: Ann Marie Forget.

In recent years, innovations like Goretex and Thinsulate have revolutionized outdoor apparel, so that outdoor clothes are now slim and fashionable as well as functional and long-lasting. These are performance-perfect clothes no one should be without.

SKIING

Five hundred years ago, skiing was considered a method of transportation rather than a sport. But when in more recent days some hardy pilgrims carried a few sets of those long, slim slats across the ocean, Americans took hold as if they were possessed.

It was a skiing aficionado named Harold Hirch who, in 1929, developed the first American ski parka, a shelter duck jacket that Hirch felt was most fashionably accompanied by Dutch-boy pants. Because this jacket was lightweight and wind- and water-repellent, it was the perfect cover-up for the slopes.

By 1934, when the first rope tow was installed at Woodstock, Vermont, the fad for skiing had grown to manic proportions, and fashion-conscious skiers, no longer comfortable in their old work clothes or heavy hunting gear, donned specially made "ski suits" of black or navy waterproofed gabardine, tricotine, or wool.

In the early 1950s, the Scandinavian sweater, which had been the status symbol at Aspen and

P*ith helmets in their natural habitat: on safari.*

Teddy Roosevelt, the father of our National Parks, knew what it took to beat around the bush. His real clothes often came from one of the greatest outdoor outfitters ever—Abercrombie and Fitch, which, sadly, closed its doors in 1977.

Never carry a bag again! Fishing vests have pockets for everything —try one for toting camera gear.

Flyfisherman Martin Hamerman at a favorite spot somewhere in New England. The hat is a classic from the original Abercrombie and Fitch, but you can still find the fisherman's vest and waders at L.L. Beans.

Vail in the forties, was replaced by a remarkable jacket designed by a devoted outdoorsman from Seattle named Eddie Bauer. Originally made in 1936 and designed for Arctic and Antarctic explorers, this quilted, goose-down cotton duck jacket provided skiers for the first time with warmth without bulk or weight. The use in the 1950s of nylon radicalized Bauer's "Skyliner" design and made his revolutionary jacket—still one of Bauer's top-selling items— even more efficient.

It was championship jumper Will Bogner and his wife Maria who first exhibited form-fitting stretch pants on the slopes. (When, shortly after their first appearance, the Bogners' hip-hugging trousers became *de rigueur*, one fashion expert noted that stretch pants were worn so tight that "if you had a dime in your pocket, you ought to be able to read the date.") These wool stretch trousers provided skiers maximum freedom of movement, and because the wool could tolerate a wide range of dyes, skiers were able, for the first time, to dress in a vast array of colors.

When Suzy Chaffee hotdogged her way down the slopes in 1968, ski fashion designers quickly realized that her flamboyant style required vivacious clothing to match. Today, skiers can dress as refulgently as they wish: silver jumpsuits, appliquéd denim, and neon-bright racing stripes are only a few of the more attractive accouterments available.

Racing stripes alone do not, however, keep a skier warm, and many a hotdogger was grateful when, in 1976, some kindhearted designer stitched insulated stretch inserts into ski jumpsuits.

Today, skiwear is technically perfect for the rugged life on the slopes, and much too expensive to stay there. If you're like me and have to run around town in all kinds of weather, consider investing in a skiers' jumpsuit. Not only will it keep you warm and dry, but it's lightweight, easy to care for, and roomy enough to fit comfortably over pants and a blouse.

HIKING AND CAMPING

In 1903, when Annie Peck, an apparently indefatigable professor at Purdue, climbed one of the world's highest mountain peaks (she ascended twenty during her lifetime), she wore "flannel undergarments, a serge waist, a wool sweater and knickerbockers and leggins of serge-green duck canvas." Peck opted for knickers because she knew bloomers would quickly grow heavy with water absorbed from foliage, and breeches would naturally be too tight at the knees. Most hikers followed Peck's example until the thirties, when fashion became less restrictive and shorts became *comme il faut*—at least for the summertime. But it took Eddie Bauer to protect winter hikers from the elements.

Bauer was determined to design clothes that would be capable of withstanding the rigorous atmospheric conditions of the

Russell Aaron is a top New York model. Our photographer spotted him one day between appointments wearing a favorite flannel shirt and carrying a backpack full of photos.

Himalayas, and by 1973, when men wearing his "Kara Koram" parka (two goose-down parkas in one), conquered Dhaulagiri, in the Himalayas, Bauer was established as one of the preeminent manufacturers of outdoor wear. He also made the first goose-down vest, a garment originally designed for bush pilots and guides based in the Arctic Circle.

Down, of course, is not the only efficient insulator of outdoor wear. An ideal shell garment called the 60/40 mountain parka was introduced by Sierra Designs in 1968. This combination parka (60 percent cotton and 40 percent nylon) is resistent to abrasion and mildew and more windproof and water-repellent than nylon alone (the nylon yarn protects the water-repellent dense cotton, while the cotton allows the garment to breathe and works within to provide greater weather resistance). And because this parka was designed by a motorcyclist, the 60/40 shell has seven well-placed pockets that can carry as much as a glove compartment or a small day pack.

Gore-tex is another excellent insulator, introduced commercially in 1976 after Bill Nicolai, a climber with a peculiar penchant for hiking in the Picket Range of Washington's North Cascades in the winter, agreed to make and test a tent for the Gore Company made of this curious-looking membrane no one else would touch. Nicolai hitched into the Cascades, set himself up in an infelicitous spot named Icicle Creek (it was 29° F.), and discovered, to his surprise, that the stuff worked: "When I woke up in the morning, I felt the side of the tent and it was bone dry. A shiver went down my spine."

Gore-tex fabric is composed of a microporous Gore-tex membrane protected on one or both sides by fabric. The membrane is made of 100 percent PTFE (polytetrafluoroethylene), or Teflon to you and me. The membrane has 9 billion pores per square inch; each pore is 700 times larger than a water vapor molecule, but thousands of times smaller than a drop of liquid water, making Gore-tex fabric both waterproof and breatheable. Because the pores are misaligned, the fabric is also windproof. This remarkable membrane can be bonded to almost any material for nearly unlimited use (including shoes, gloves, and outerwear). Perhaps best of all, Gore-tex fabric is completely machine-washable.

Anyone interested in a securely insulated garment that will provide warmth and mobility without bulk should investigate garments made with Thinsulate. Thinsulate is a remarkable innovation recently introduced by the 3M Company. This unique microfiber insulation (65 percent olefin and 35 percent polyester) is breatheable, hypoallergenic, and can be hand- or machine-washed without bunching or matting. Because Thinsulate fibers absorb less than 1 percent of their weight in water, a garment made with Thinsulate will keep you warm even in damp conditions. And because

Thinsulate is available in different thicknesses, it is easily adapted for a variety of uses, including boots, gloves, jackets, vests, and rainwear.

FIELD AND STREAM

When, in 1912, a Down East hunter named Leon Leonwood Bean got tired of traipsing about the woods with wet, cold feet, he worked himself a pair of funny-looking lace-up boots with rubber bottoms and leather tops. L. L. liked his boots so much that he decided to sell them to other like-minded fellows, and within five years, the dry-footed entrepreneur had to move out of his brother's confining haberdashery and into a larger building across the road on Main Street in Portland, Maine, where the retail store of the now famous L. L. Bean Company still stands.

The Bean Company is still selling the original hunting shoe (in a variety of styles, priced anywhere from about $41 to $78) and nearly 2,500 other good-looking, well-made items, including chamois shirts, flannel nightshirts, chino shorts, down vests, and even, for men and women, a neck-tie dotted with tiny but distinctly recognizable hunting shoes. Many Bean items can be used for multiple purposes; for example, their handwoven split-willow fisherman's creel can be used as a great-looking and capacious haversack, book bag, or gym bag.

The Woolrich Company of Pennsylvania is another superior manufacturer of classic American outdoor gear. Woolrich was established by an Englishman named John Rich who in 1830 had the prescience to build his wool mill smack dab in the middle of one of the prime lumbering areas of the time. It was to satisfy both the professional and recreational needs of the incipient lumberjack population that Rich designed his now famous red-and-black plaid hunting suit, still considered by many to be the "most quiet coat and pants ever worn through the woods."

During the beginning of the twentieth century, it was Abercrombie & Fitch (aka the F. A. O. Schwarz for adults) who provided Teddy Roosevelt and other members of the *fin de siècle* leisure class with the gear required for African safaris, cocktail parties, and other like adventures. Abercrombie & Fitch's beautifully tailored green, beige, brown, and heather gabardines were found to be both inconspicuous in the woods and tasteful at the club. In 1977, when Abercrombie & Fitch closed, Hunting World took over, and this nationally known store continues to provide adventure seekers and the fashion-conscious with elegant, superbly crafted safari suits, hats, elephant-hair bracelets, and explorers' bags.

RIDING

Like almost every other article of riding apparel, equestrians' coats evolved from British hunting clothing. Each point of tailoring

Almost everyone has seen this catalog at one time or another, since Leon Leonwood Bean started mailing them in 1912. Back then the sole product was hunting shoes, now they have everything for the outdoors.

A *British hunting outfit from 1842 features the very same boots that English style riders wear today.*

Jockey's *goggles from H. Kauffman Saddlery are extremely lightweight (they have to be—jockeys sometimes wear as many as six pairs during a race run on a sloppy track, constantly pulling a clean pair over their eyes). Try them for a really sleek look.*

had a specific functional purpose: The long skirts that interfered with comfortable riding were cut away; the pockets were slanted to permit easier accessibility when riding; the flap covers on the pockets were added to prevent hankies and other bits of paraphernalia from flying out and to keep rain from saturating the contents; and the storm tab allowed the coat to enclose the rider against the elements. Traditionally, riding coats were made of wool, but because polyester, dacron, and rayon increase wear, improve fit, and make the garment easier to clean, coats made of these fabrics have recently gained popularity.

When the British went to India and discovered that tall boots were unbearably uncomfortable in the hot climate, they elongated the tapered three-quarter-length leg of the traditional riding breeches into cuff-bottomed or flare-bottomed jodhpurs that could be worn with cooler ankle-high boots. Both jodhpurs and traditional breeches are designed to prevent chafing and withstand the stress of mounting and dismounting.

Riding boots originated in the seventeenth century and were first made of grain leather. The flesh inner side was left brown and the outside was blackened and polished to a dull finish. When the flesh side was turned down, it formed a cuff that evolved into the brown-topped boot worn by today's jockeys. Tall riding boots are designed to be worn with breeches, but they are sure to add a touch of class to any wardrobe. If you do splurge on a pair, make sure the heels slip slightly; unlike shoes, boots will tighten across the heel with use.

A silk jockey blouse can also add panache to your wardrobe. Although these blouses are somewhat expensive, they're stitched to last a lifetime and they make an unforgettable fashion statement.

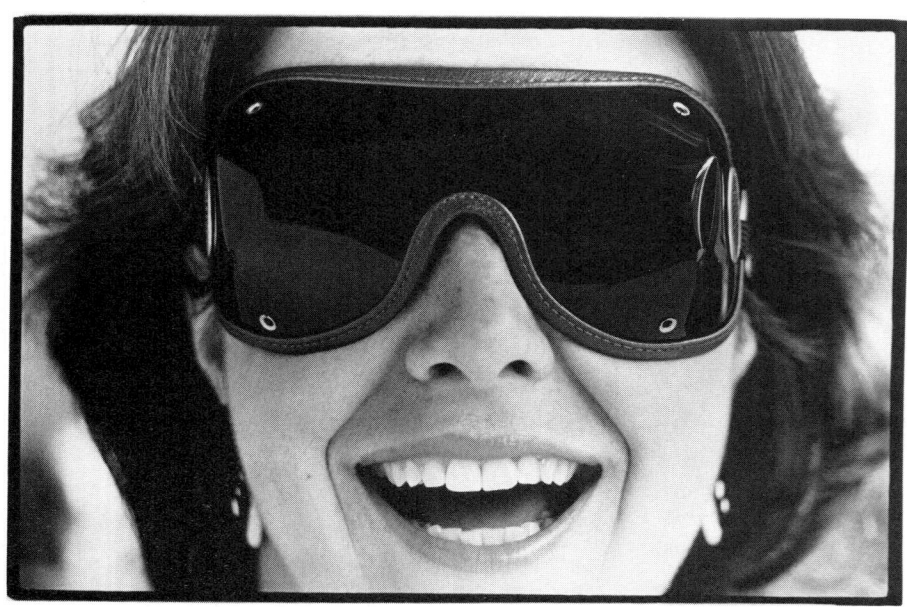

A luxurious and sporty silk jockey's shirt can add an elegant flair to your wardrobe. Worn by Ann Marie Forget.

Inset: when the winter winds whip into town, snuggle into this wool knit "tube" that fashions as a hood or a cowl. From French Creek Sheep and Wool.

Imported from the East, these warm wool and rayon gloves are knit by native women in Afghanistan. Colors and patterns vary with the maker so no two pairs of these vibrant handwarmers are exactly alike Early Winters (see Index) thinks you'll like them, or you get your money back.

56 Real Clothes

On this page: a bright shiny nylon jumpsuit for skiing. It features a collar that can be drawn up to protect half the face. Right: Wonderful examples of the shirt-style down filled ski "anorak" by the Italian manufacturer Colmar. They're handled in the U.S. by Wasco (see Index). Check their catalog for page after page of sleek surprises for the "anti-conformist skier."

Woolrich Bib Overalls. Heavy, warm, water repellant 30 oz wool makes these gray and red bib overalls absolutely unbeatable in winter. Available from Eastern Mountain Sports.

Real Clothes 59

We can't say it any better —here's what the Deerskin Trading Post writes: "In handsome gray tweed ragg wool, these gloves are very functional for shooting sports and winter chores. They leave thumb and fingers free for precision movement, while your hands stay toasty warm."

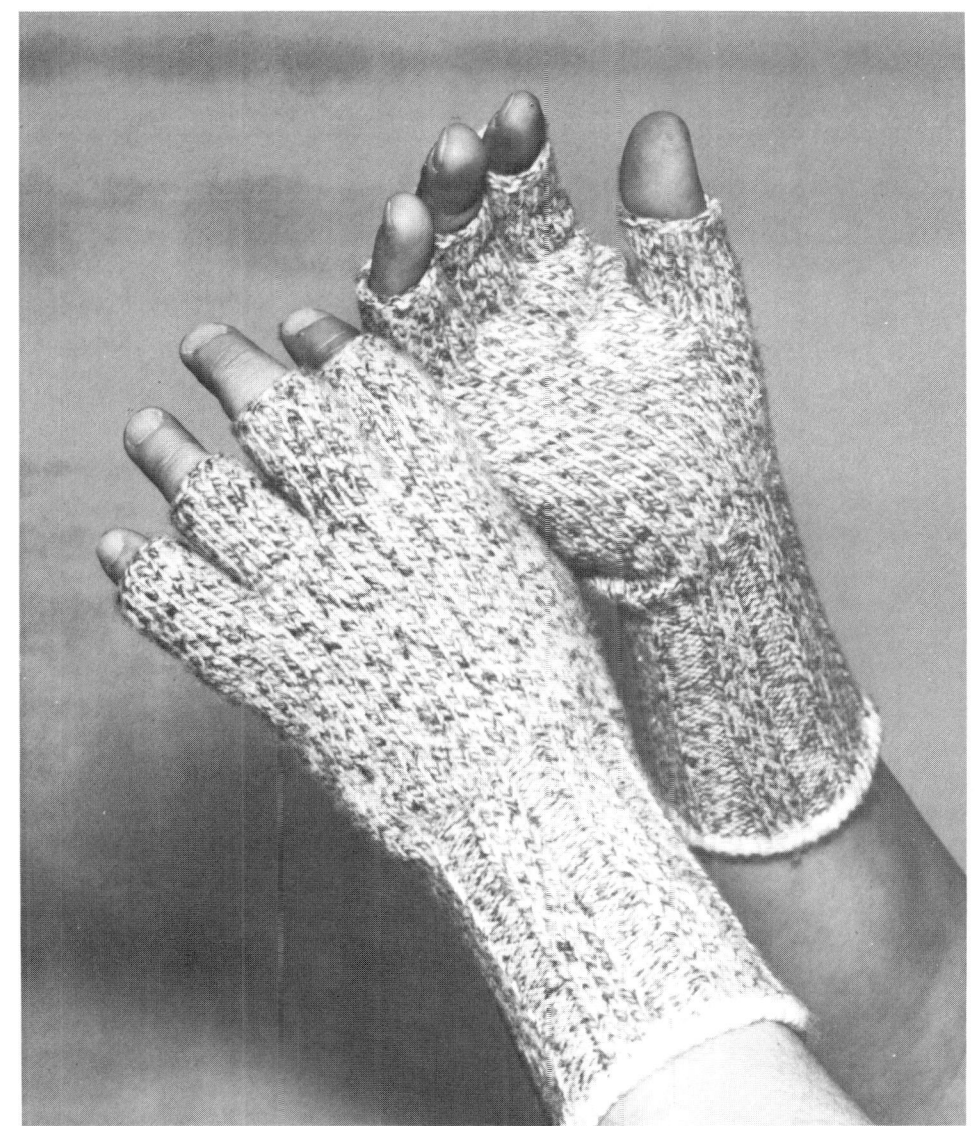

The catalog from Banana Republic is full of wonderful clothes and accessories made from cotton in all its incarnations: lightweight Egyptian cotton, cotton poplin and cotton twill (poplin is finely ribbed, medium heavy, while twill has a diagonal weave so fine it's hard to see), jersey knit cotton, cotton canvas . . . . even a few items made from wool. See the Index.

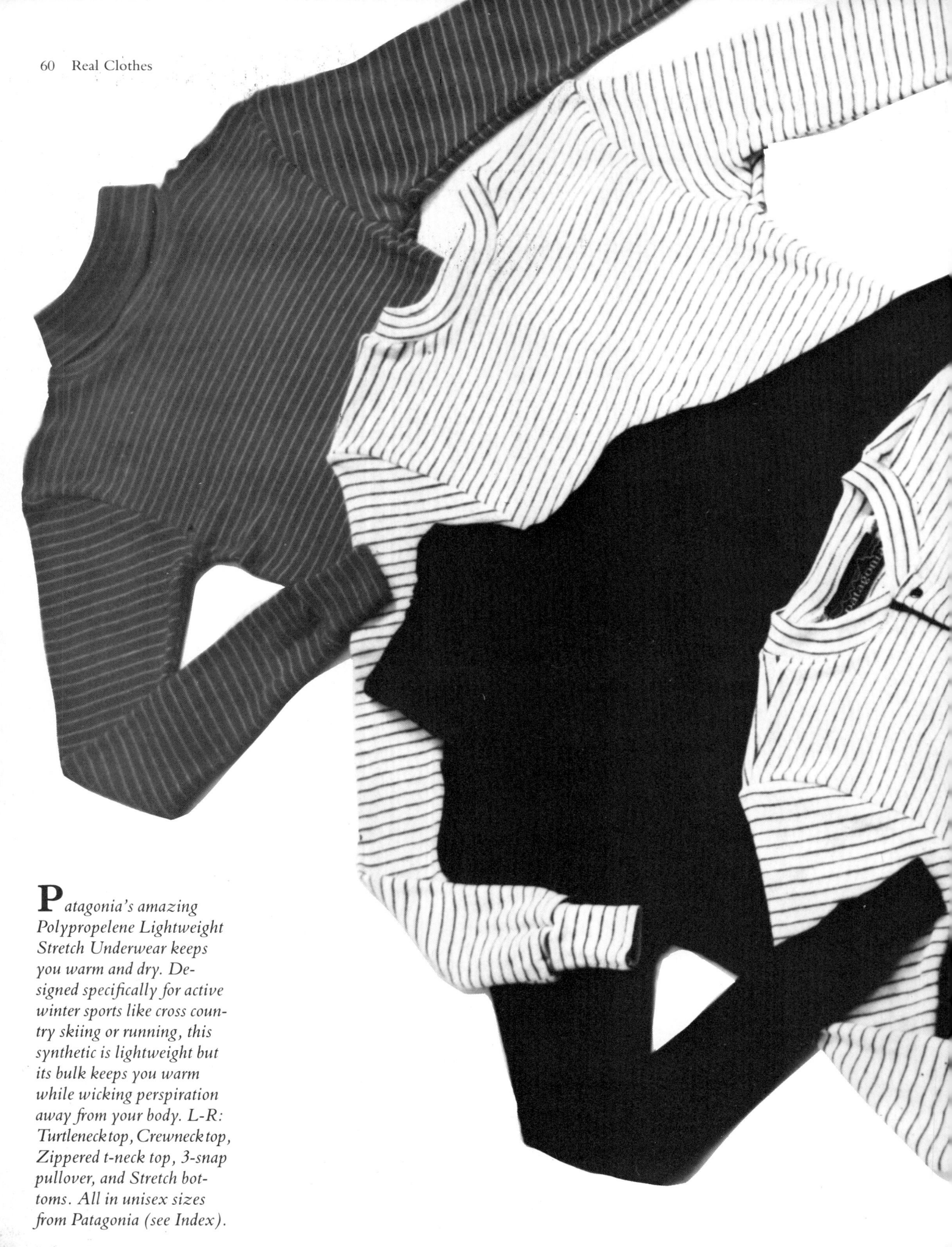

60 Real Clothes

Patagonia's amazing Polypropelene Lightweight Stretch Underwear keeps you warm and dry. Designed specifically for active winter sports like cross country skiing or running, this synthetic is lightweight but its bulk keeps you warm while wicking perspiration away from your body. L-R: Turtleneck top, Crewneck top, Zippered t-neck top, 3-snap pullover, and Stretch bottoms. All in unisex sizes from Patagonia (see Index).

Real Clothes 61

This plain wool reversible jacket is insulated. Buttons up the front, has a large warm stand-up collar. From Antler.

Blazing Orange nylon canvas jacket and pants insulated with dacron Hollofil. This color is so loud you'll be seen and heard. From Antler.

Bop but don't drop in genuine leather boxing shoes from Pony.

4

Sportschic

*hockey jerseys • cyclists' gloves
• warm-up suits • baseball
jackets • boxers' robes*

At the turn of the century women were sometimes arrested for baring their ankles at the beach, but by the time Johnny Weissmuller and diving champion Aileen Riggen made their splash in 1930, the authorities could tolerate a bit more skin.

The precise demands of athletic activity have demanded a certain constancy in sports uniforms. As a result, men's uniforms have seen little change during the past century.

A number of sartorial innovations that facilitate better performance have, however, been responsible for some changes in sports uniforms. The zipper, for example, a handy little device invented by Whitcomb L. Judson in the 1890s, was first used on sports uniforms, as was Velcro tape. Even the homely snap fastener was designed to ensure a buckaroo's hasty escape if his shirt, just by chance, happened to be caught on a bull's horn.

Women's sports uniforms, on the other hand, have undergone radical changes since the days when female athletes were constrained by "armour that clasped us tightly in all sorts of agonizing places." Until relatively recently, women were ridiculed for their participation in sports; it was only forty-five years ago that Paul Gallico, a columnist for *Vogue*, wrote: "Out of a list of some twenty-five sports, in which ladies of to-day indulge with vehemence and passion—and also, it is to be noted with regret, in public—there are only nine in which they do not manage to look utterly silly." Those tolerated by Mr. Gallico were archery, backstroke swimming, figure skating, riding, skiing, speed skating, aviation, shooting, and angling. Badminton and other sports were

responsible for, among other unpleasantries, "moustaches of perspiration on their lips." When women became accustomed to open-air exercise, however, they refused to "endure excessively tight, heavy, unhygienic clothing," and gradually women's uniforms began to parallel the fine design of men's.

CYCLING

Cycling was the first sport to gain mass appeal in America. By the 1890s, even the most modest woman was compelled to reveal her ankles if she was to enjoy the sport.

It was an engaging and feisty woman named Amelia Jenkins Bloomer who revolutionized cycling clothes. Resenting the plethora of undergarments women were required to wear when exercising (five to ten petticoats, a camisole, and a corset with stays, which, let it be known, often caused fainting and dislodged organs, was not unusual), Bloomer stripped off her long skirts and stitched up a pair of "bloomers." This voluminous but eminently more practical garment did not at least get caught in the spokes.

In the thirties, when the Depression forced our automobile-loving culture back to its bikes, the culotte, a garment with the "comfort of trousers, the grace of a skirt," was introduced; two decades later, the culotte was transformed into pedal pushers.

Today, professional cyclists wear skintight wool, cotton, or polyester/wool–blend shorts that provide the maximum in comfort and style. Sergal, one of the best-known manufacturers of cyclists' gear, makes a great-looking, long-tailed wool jersey that's perfect active wear for anyone who wants a sharp, racy look. Other manufacturers make jerseys of cotton and nylon—the nylon is on the outside, where it provides protection against the elements, the cotton is next to the skin for comfort. Arm warmers convert a short-sleeved jersey into a warmer long-sleeved one and can be used by anyone as a whimsical and unexpected fashion accessory. Cyclists' gloves, most often made of leather and crocheted cotton, also make a surprising and cool-looking accessory.

SWIMMING

In the late nineteenth century, women who wanted to enjoy the pleasures of sand and surf wore outfits similar to Bloomer's cycling outfits. These heavy garments were rather troublesome, to say the least, when water-soaked. It took professional swimmer Annette Kellerman, who preferred the knit woollen one-piece bathing suit worn by men, presenting herself in a man's suit to His Majesty Edward II, to change the course of swimsuit fashion (Kellerman did, at the last minute, agree to wear black stockings beneath her outfit.) By the way, although the king was not offended, when Kellerman strolled along the beaches of Boston in her revolutionary suit, she was arrested.

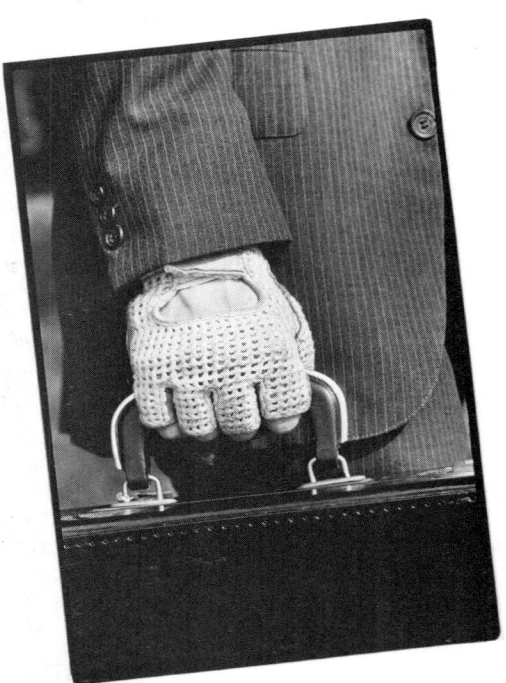

Pinstripes two ways. Above, David Skalak's cycling gloves make his ride to work more comfortable—they're fingerless for ease of movement and the padded leather palms provide cushioning. Opposite, Joltin' Joe DiMaggio wearing the functional and famous Yankee pinstriped uniform.

Worn over the traditional daily uniform, New York Attorney David Skalak's cycling items are more than mere accessories after the fact—they add comfort and protection.

Fireman Steve Casse about to blaze homeward. The wool shorts and knit cotton jersey fit snugly to cut down wind resistance, and cycling shoes provide a perfect fit in the bicycles toe clips.

Opposite: Pele, the world's most famous soccer player, wearing the uniform of the New York Cosmos. At the height of his career, the Brazilian athlete was considered a national treasure.

When the Jantzen Company introduced their relatively abbreviated "swimsuit" (as opposed to the formerly worn "bathing outfits") in 1921, the tan became the newest status symbol. While enthusiastically worn by fashionable women, this flapper-style suit offended the authorities; plainclothes policewomen patrolled the beaches with measuring sticks to make sure that a woman's outfit was never higher than six inches above the knee.

In the 1930s, Lastex, "the miracle yarn that makes things fit," changed the look of swimsuits almost as much as Kellerman had. Shirred cotton sewn with Lastex thread was available in more colors and patterns than the traditional wool, but most importantly it allowed swimsuits to be for the first time nearly form-fitting.

Since the thirties, we've seen women abandon the midriff-style suit in favor of the pinup-girl style (designed to "glamorize your curves"), and then in the sixties adopt Jacques Heim's innovation, the bikini. It's been said that the next thing to come is a fabric that can be penetrated by ultraviolet light so that no matter what you wear, you'll be guaranteed an allover tan.

What will they think in Boston?

TENNIS

In 1877, a *Punch* cartoonist suggested that men who were interested in playing an equal game with women be handicapped by tying scarves around their knees. It seems that neither the ubiquitous bustle nor the corset was conducive to a proper backhand.

And yet the physical constraints imposed on women were only gradually relaxed on the court. In 1904, May Sutton, the first American to win at Wimbledon, helped the process when she scandalized both the judges and audience by rolling up her sleeves.

But it took a Frenchwoman, the daring Suzanne Langlen, to really revolutionize tennis gear. When she appeared at Wimbledon in 1919, she swaggered onto the court in a simple calf-length cotton frock, worn most obviously without petticoats or corsets. Reporters were quick to pronounce her "the French hussy," but when she won the title, her outfit was adopted worldwide.

It was the aptly named Teddy Tinling who was responsible for the next great change in women's tennis wear. Tinling found flimsy tunics designed to barely cover the derriere just the thing for tennis pros, and tennis pros apparently thought the same, for during the forties and fifties, female tennis stars wore Tinling-designed gold lamé panties or flower-print hot pants beneath their nylon sheers. Today, Tinling is still helping glamorize the stars: When Billie Jean King trounced Bobby Riggs a few years back, she was wearing a Tinling-designed costume with a bodice insert decorated with hundreds of sequins and rhinestones.

Helen Wills Moody, the winner of thirty-one titles, is credited

The famous Fred Perry, wearing the traditional tennis garb of the 1930's.

with sporting the first tennis visor in 1927, a snappy-looking and extremely functional device great for wear on or off the courts.

JOGGING

Although people have been jogging for decades, it took Jack Kennedy and his national physical fitness program to really get Americans running. Within a remarkably short time, folks all over the country realized that regular jogging defends against heart attacks, remedies low blood pressure, and effects a failsafe cure for insomnia. By the late seventies, there were over 160 styles of running shoes available, made in colors the rainbow never even heard of. And don't forget warm-up suits. They're made in everything from acrylic to cotton and are great for shopping, pre-exercise exercise, or just plain lounging around.

TEAM UNIFORMS

Since most sports uniforms are priced for schools or teams, they make a real fashion value.

Inexpensive football pants, for example, mold like a second skin (the inside pockets can be removed for a neater fit). Or try wearing a football jersey alone as a minidress. Baseball jackets, available in nylon, cotton, satin, and leather, are colorful, casual, and make a comfortable complement to almost any outfit. Try wearing stirrup socks with a miniskirt—they make an unforgettable accessory. A hockey jersey can be worn as a tunic (try it with the V in the back), or as a smooth and silky blouse. Basketball uniforms are cool and versatile—try wearing a basketball jersey with stovepipe pants tucked into something totally unexpected, like dancers' slippers. A soccer jersey with its white-gusseted V-neck collar and cuffs is a multipurpose classic. Goalie jerseys, made with quilted elbows, are an excellent choice for skaters. Black-and-white vertically striped referee jerseys and jackets make a classic, graphic fashion statement. And remember Muhammad Ali in his red velvet shorts with the white stripes and the robe to match? Well, why not? A boxer's three-quarter-length satin robe with the collar, belt, and cuffs in contrasting colors makes a great lounge robe or a terrific evening cover-up.

74　Real Clothes

Gearing up. Danielle Sacripante, an artist for a New York advertising agency, tops out in a dyed surplus "air policeman's cap cover" and an all-nylon reversible baseball jacket which she found at a local surplus store.

Right: New York artist's agent Sallie Mars decked out in a straw "boater" and a personal favorite—her sturdy cotton rugby shirt that keeps going and going. Even after 10 years it feels better with every washing.

When Stuart Bragg's father lettered in crew at Princeton in 1944, he received this heavy wool sweater. Stuart doesn't row, but wearing this he's already a few lengths ahead. Photographed at Cafe Reginette, New York City.

Magazine editor Pearl Sverdlin in a cotton hooded snap-front cardigan and matching pants. This sports inspired outfit was designed by Adrienne Vittadini. Courtesy Charivari Sport, New York City.

78 Real Clothes

From SUB-4, top of the line, head of the pack running gear. Many of their shorts have a handy inside change and key pocket, while the tops (called singlets) are super lightweight nylon, nylon mesh, or cotton-nylon blends for comfort and breathability.

Real Clothes 81

Coat sweaters in wool or orlon with warm hoods. Sweater on the right has drawstring waist for a snug, warm fit. From Cheerleader Supply Company.

From the Performance Bicycle Shop, check out this quality lightweight rainwear of Antron Nylon. The versatile rainsuit features a vented jacket and an adjustable hood. The pants have vertical zippered closures and an elastic waistband. The poncho's hood has a visor to keep the rain out, and outside drawstrings pull the hood snugly around the face.

Bicyclist's trim riding shorts made of wool, cotton, or cotton/polyester provide the maximum in comfort and streamlined style.
From Performance Bicycle Shop

Accessorized! Cyclists hats come in dozens of colors, usually with a neat professional name silkscreened on to advertise an equipment brand. Here one's worn with mountaineering glasses available from Hudsons. Try the Performance Bicycle Shop for hats under five dollars.

84 Real Clothes

Accessories in every color or pattern imaginable come from the NFL Merchandise Catalog (as in the case of these hats) or Cheerleader's Supply (make yourself a letter sweater.)

Nylon tube socks with elastic turn-down cuffs are inexpensive and you can order them from Cheerleader Supply Company in your choice of colors and complementary strips.

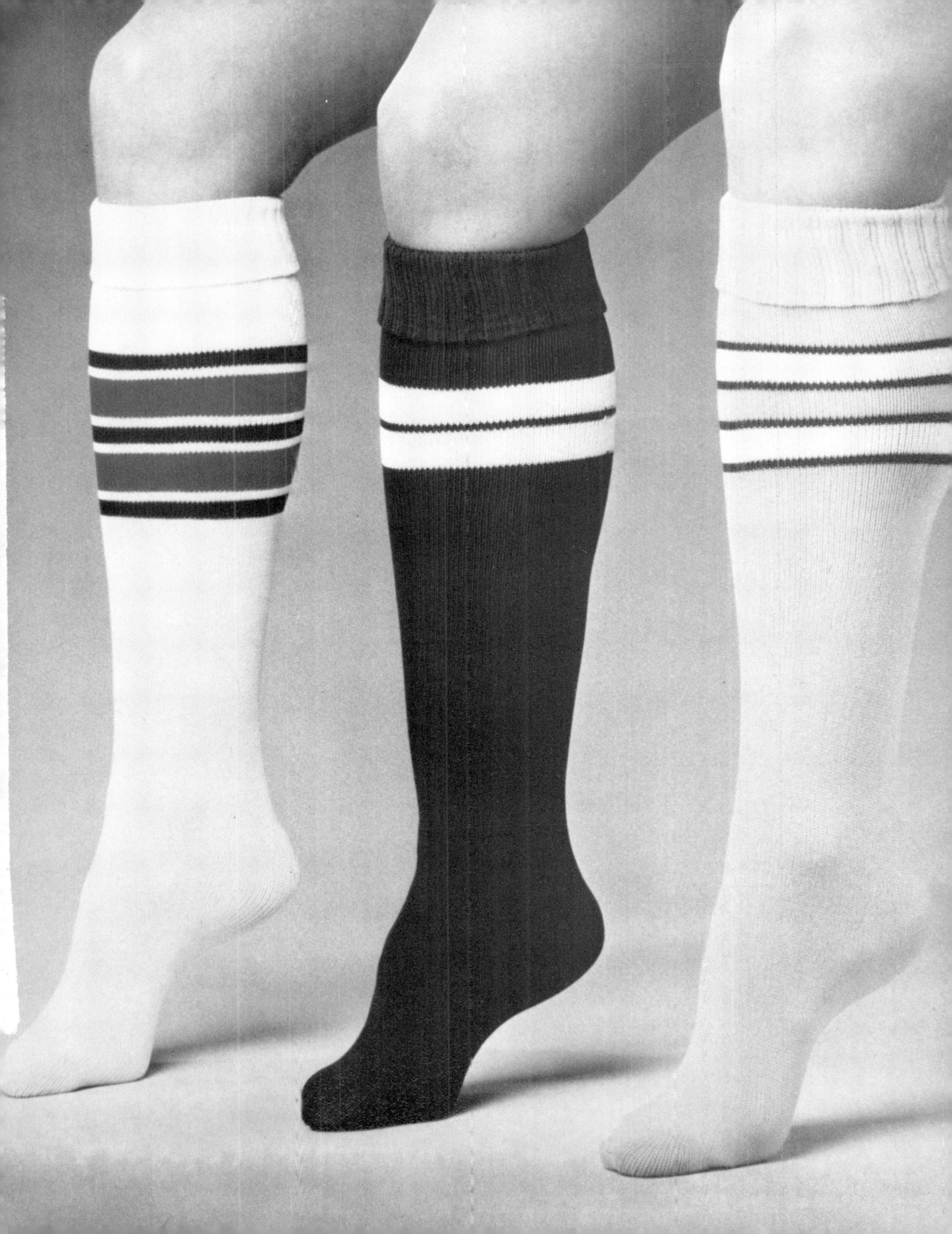

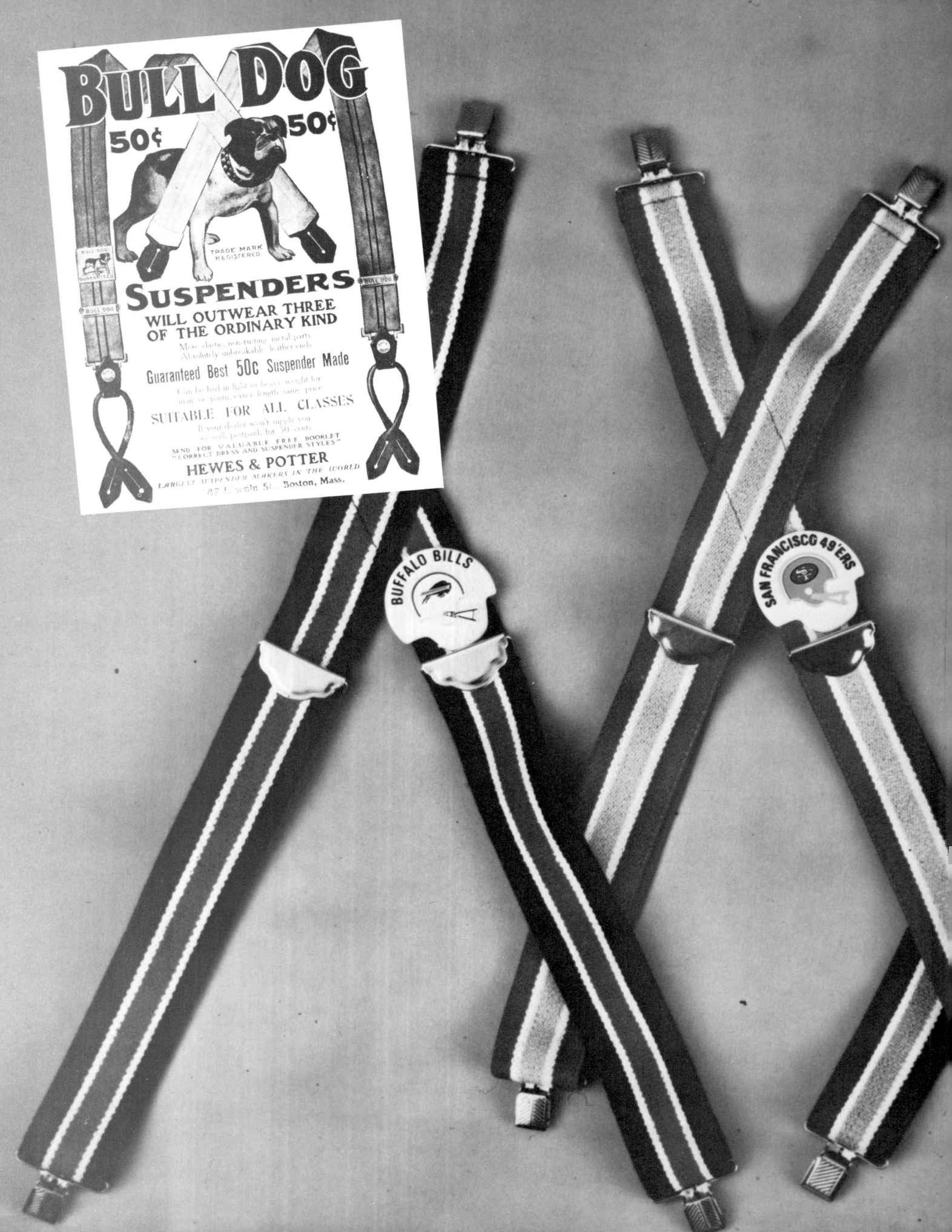

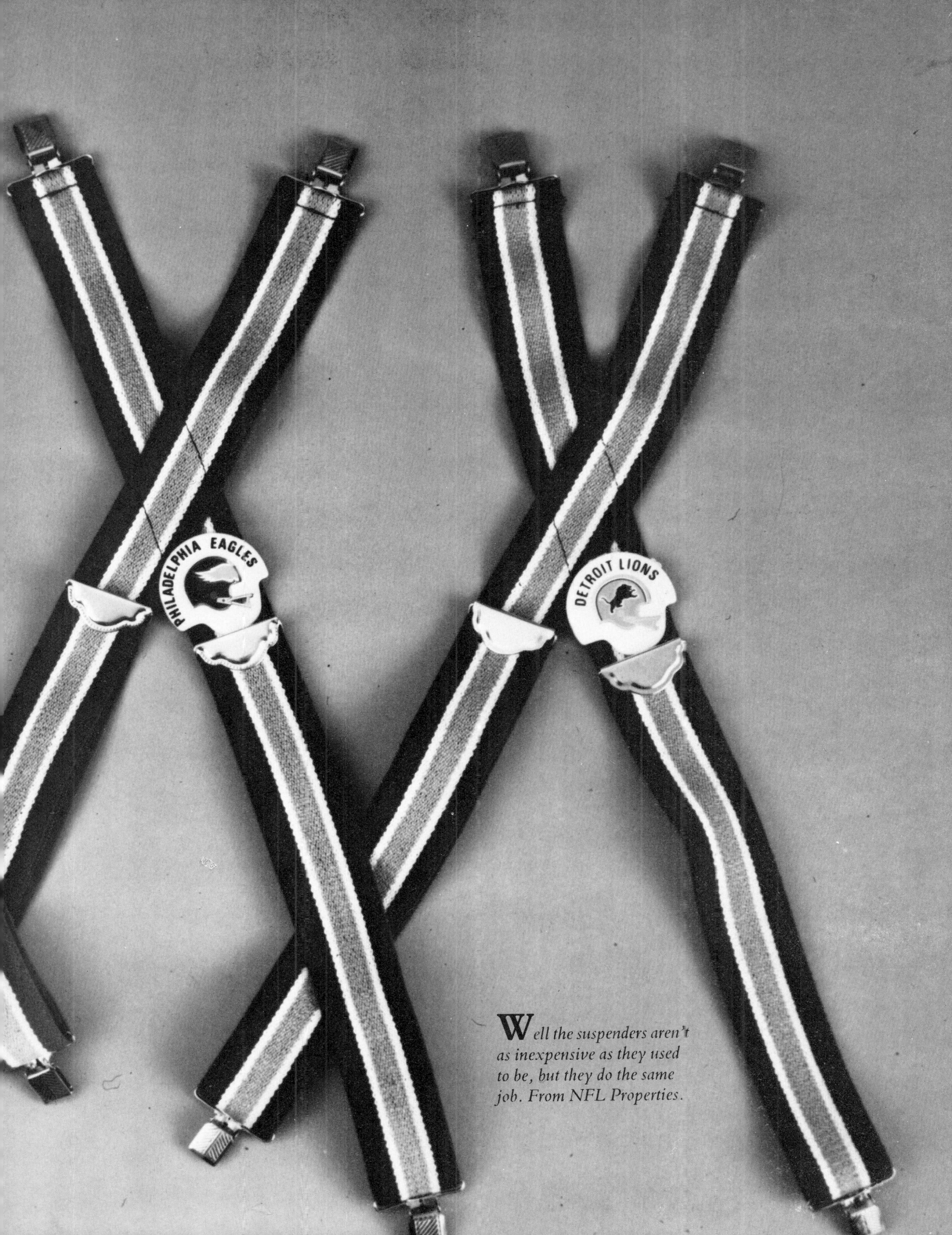

CARL EMERY GIORDANO

Any time of day or night, this "turn-out gear" is ready to go at Manhattan's Great Jones Street firehouse.

5
ACTION-TESTED FASHION
rainwear • suspenders • attack coats • boots

Below, a New York University security staff sargeant.

Police and firefighter uniforms must satisfy three basic criteria: First, they must be highly protective; second, they must be affordable; and third, they must provide durability and warmth without weight. Today's superbly designed uniforms do just that; what's more, they're styled along classic lines, which means they can easily transformed into your perennial fashion favorites.

POLICE

So accustomed are we to seeing uniformed civil servants that it's hard to imagine a time when police and firefighters did not wear specially identifying clothing. But in about 1650, when Peter Stuyvesant organized the first police force of New Amsterdam, his officials wore naught but their ordinary street clothes. Because these men were equipped solely with small gourdlike devices containing pebbles, they were referred to, rather disingenuously, as the Rattle Watch.

It wasn't until 1693 then that the first uniformed police officer walked the streets of New York. This single dutiful gentleman was known as the bellman, and it was decreed by the city legislators that he be provided with "a coat of ye citty livery with a badge of ye citty arms, and shoes and stockings." And so he was.

By 1803, the City Watch had expanded to 140 men, many of whom wore leather hats similar in

Sister, can you spare a dime? Police used to wear a star shaped copper shield pinned to their jackets —hence the term "cops."

The Kittatinny Hose Company of Newark, N.J., photographed in 1882. By the late nineteenth century, firefighter's hats had evolved from what had been a typical narrow brimmed stovepipe hat into what we now know as the classic firefighter's helmet. The enlarged brim protects the men from falling debris, and also keeps the water from running down their backs.

This New York City traffic cop stays warm in his policeman's "dress reefer coat" of heavy nylon twill.

design to a modern firefighter's helmet and a caped overcoat. When the ever-increasing din of the nineteenth century made rattles obsolete, officers began carrying more intimidating and formidable sticks.

As the burgeoning industrialism of the century brought not just noise but crime, in 1844, the City Watch system was abandoned and replaced by the more militaristic Municipal Police Force. It was during this year that the mayor made his first attempt to uniform a single corps of officers. At the time, though, neither officers nor the citizens—who referred to their uniformed protectors as "liveried lackeys"—were very well disposed to the idea, and so, with the inauguration of the next mayor, not only the uniforms but the entire corps was abolished. For a few years, then, the only official insignia permitted was a star-shaped copper shield worn pinned to the jacket (hence the designation "cops").

During the next ten years, the battle of the uniforms continued. Some officers felt that a uniform added to the individual's sense of self-respect, while others felt the imposition of regulated clothing degraded their manhood. While many private citizens continued to oppose the uniforms, others complained that the lack of identifying clothing jeopardized their safety. It took the forceful persuasion of a stylish young commissioner to end the debate: After pointing out that, left to their own devices, the members of the force looked—on their good days—rather raggedy and disreputable, a uniform was adopted.

The uniform of the mid-1850s consisted of a blue coat with a velvet collar and brass buttons, a cloth cap, and gray pants with black stripes down both outside seams. By 1875, when the city was experiencing the first dire effects of rampant industrialism, the flat-topped cap was replaced by a helmet and the officers were armed with clubs.

The various kinds of uniforms worn by today's police range from the rather imposing-looking if relatively soft gray Stetsons worn in parts of the South to the "ballistic-defeating equipment" and "task-effective armor" worn by police in many cities.

The technologically advanced rainwear worn by many police is some of the best protective outerwear available. The rugged, lightweight, machine-washable raincoats are designed for a neat fit, but they are also cut wide enough to allow circulation and easy access to equipment. And because they must keep an officer dry even in a downpour, they are treated with polyurethane, neoprene, or another highly water-repellent substance, and most have specially sealed seams and rustproof snap fasteners. Best of all, many are reversible and can be worn with the dark side out on demure days, the fluorescent orange or red side out during occasions that call for less reserve.

L-R Patrick Holahan, Bill Tanzosh, Steve Hickey, and Bill Van Wart, firefighters with Engine Company 16 and Ladder Company 7 in New York City wearing their "attack coats." Fireman Tanzosh, kneeling, with an oxygen tank which provides a fresh breathing supply in case of dense smoke.

This raincoat by clothing designer Arthur Smith for his label, "Artie and Cheech" was inspired by the policeman's raincoat below. It's worn by art dealer Ira Resnick.

FIREFIGHTERS

America's first fire company was organized in 1736 in Philadelphia at the behest of our own Prometheus, Benjamin Franklin. Although Franklin's firefighters did not at first wear distinctive clothing, most of the men did sport one immortal accessory: gallowses, or, as they're known today, suspenders.

It was apparently Jacob Turck, a gunsmith and Overseer of Fire Engines in New York City, who, in the middle of the eighteenth century, devised the first round firefighter's hat, which he made of stovepipe and shaped with a narrow brim. However, Turck left it to an ingenious soul in the nineteenth century to design the rearward extension that so effectively protects firefighters from water and falling debris.

Because fire departments were volunteer organizations until 1865, fighters were not required to wear official uniforms. However, left to their own devices, these feisty volunteers quickly developed a reputation for wearing gorgeous if not downright outlandish frippery. Indeed, despite the fact that fire laddies returned from the job in a "sadly grimed and bedraggled condition," there was not a man among them who in 1820 would be seen without his white duck shirt and black leather belt. Canvas capes treated by the owner with at least three layers of creatively brushed paint were also considered *de rigueur* by nineteenth-century firefighters.

Like many members of the police force, the first paid fire department in New York resisted standardized clothing. Indeed, many of the members threatened to resign before they would wear "livery." To quell the mutiny, commissioners began wearing uniforms, and gradually the obstreperous joined the ranks and donned the prescribed outfit.

Some New York City fire companies, however, had adopted uniform coats of heavy drab kersey with large side pockets and oversized white bone buttons as early as the 1830s. The trousers worn by these men were made of the same material and were designed, the purchaser was assured, with a waistband "made to button quick." The red flannel or wool shirts worn by some of these firefighters until just after the Civil War are still available today; combined with black leather pants, they make an impressive fashion statement.

Although attractive, the first official uniforms did not facilitate work; it has only been in the 20th century that uniform manufacturers have developed clothing that is both protective and durable and that permits maximum mobility. A firefighter's three-quarter-length jacket (aka an "attack coat") is one of the most handsomely designed and attractive jackets around. This lightweight coat, designed with a wide bellows-type sleeve and smart-looking corduroy collar, has reinforced pockets with snap-down flaps and a bright

Scotchlite reflective trim. Best of all, there's a waterproof layer of wool on the inside of the cuff to keep rain from tickling your wrists. Or try a pair of knee-high firefighters' boots. The thick grip sole of these hardy boots provides the ultimate in safety, and the Scotchlite trim gives them an extra touch of whimsy.

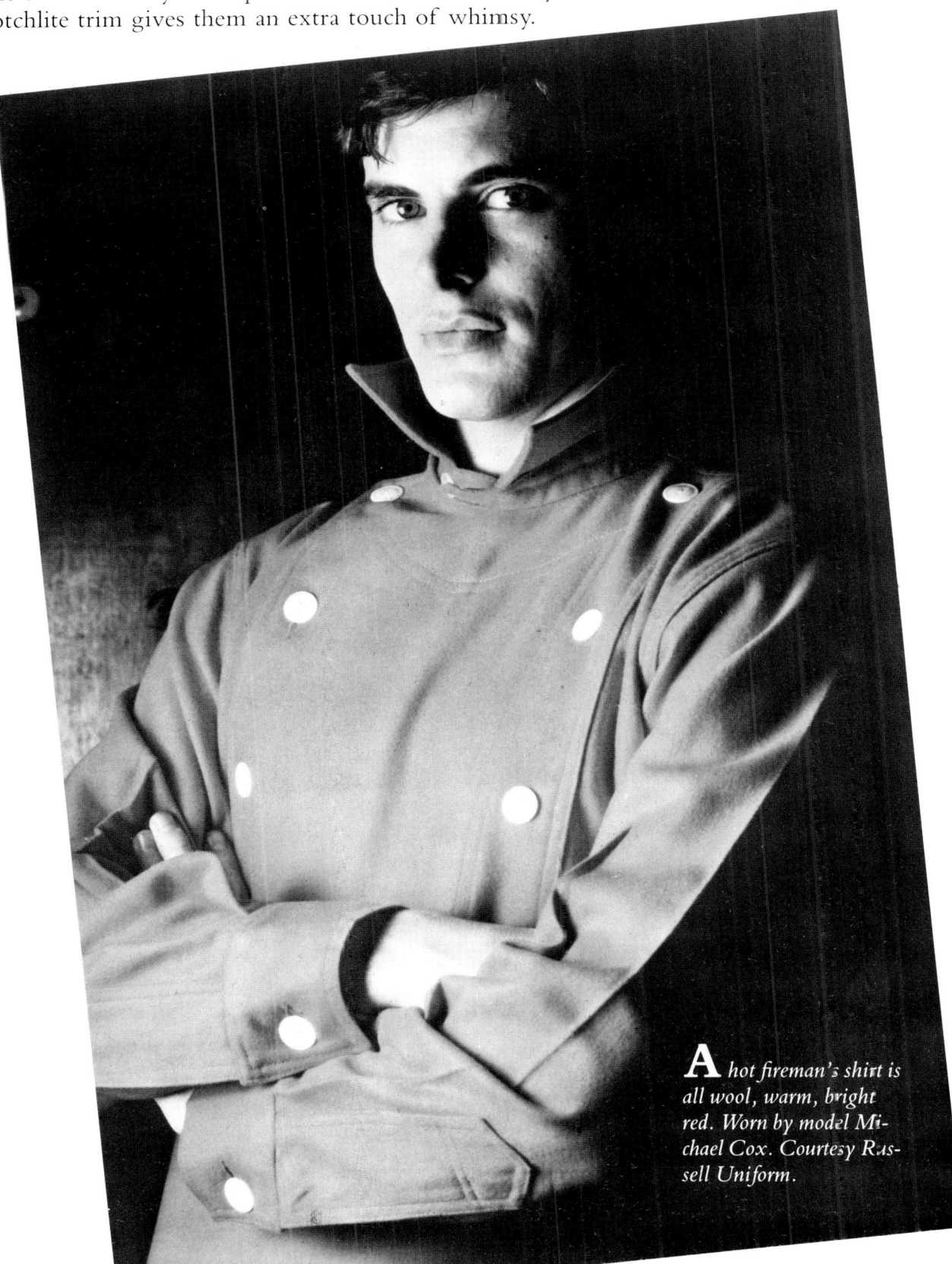

A hot fireman's shirt is all wool, warm, bright red. Worn by model Michael Cox. Courtesy Russell Uniform.

98 Real Clothes

She'll stop traffic—model Jeri LeShay in an eye-catching safety-yellow policeman's raincoat. Hat, coat, and gloves are available from Russell Uniform.

Model Frank Campisano in a bright yellow police slicker. These raincoats won't leak, peel, stiffen, or get tacky—and you can find them in colors you wouldn't expect —forest green, black, or flourescent orange. To stay super dry add waterproof leggings. Available from Blauer's and I. Buss.

Blauer's MX-V Convertible Jacket is just about the last word in practical versatility. Available in police blue and incorporating a flourescent orange safety vest, this jacket features a pop-out hood, removable pile collar, leather trimmed slash pockets, deep breast pockets, leather trimmed cuffs that stand up to years of hard use without fraying, zippered side vents, and much much more. Write to Blauer's for information.

This 100% nylon bomber jacket is fleece lined and comes in green or navy. From Antler.

Great over a sweater or under a lightweight shell, this down vest from Antler features patch pockets with velcro closures.

Men's quilted vest is insulated with Polyester Fiberfill. Outer and inner linings are nylon. Stand-up collar and patch pockets make this a good bet for early autumn in-between days.

A *reversible Air Force style flight jacket that flips to 100% safety orange nylon when you want to be seen. From Antler.*

The doctor is in: 100% cotton scrub suits make great p.j.'s. Or use them for exercise, or as cool summer cover-ups. Models: Frank Campisano and Kathleen Giordano.

6

Medical Magic

scrub suits • *smocks* • *capes* • *nurses' shoes*

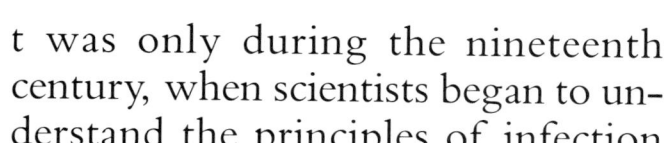

It was only during the nineteenth century, when scientists began to understand the principles of infection and prevention, that medical uniforms were designed to protect both the patient and worker from contagion. The practical and comfortable medical uniforms made today are designed not only to ensure proper hygiene but to ease the health-care professional's hectic daily schedule. That means they must be strong enough to survive frequent washings yet comfortable enough to be worn around the clock. As such, they're perfect for any active person interested in a fresh, clean look.

SURGEONS

Until the twelfth century, surgical practice was almost completely confined to the clergy, operations being occasionally assisted by the local *coiffeur*. After all, he or she did possess, if not the finesse, at least the implements to facilitate the procedure. But when, in 1163, the pope decreed that monks were no longer permitted to practice medicine, surgery was left in the willing if dubious hands of the barbers.

These rather versatile if questionable "barber-surgeons" committed their practice unhindered through the middle of the eighteenth century, and dressed throughout the centuries in a manner not unlike their contemporaries. It seems that their particular kind of work called for little more sar-

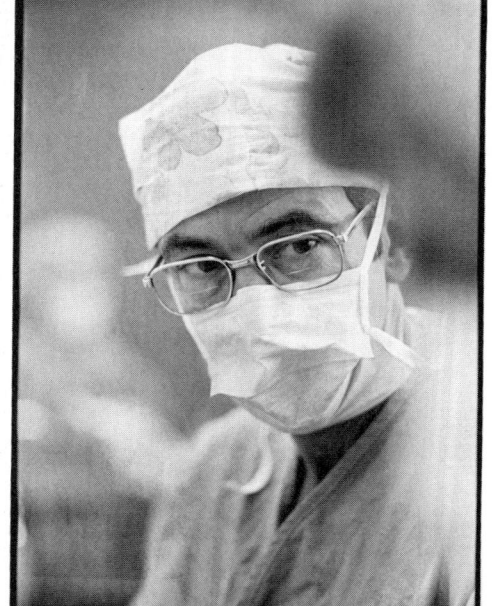

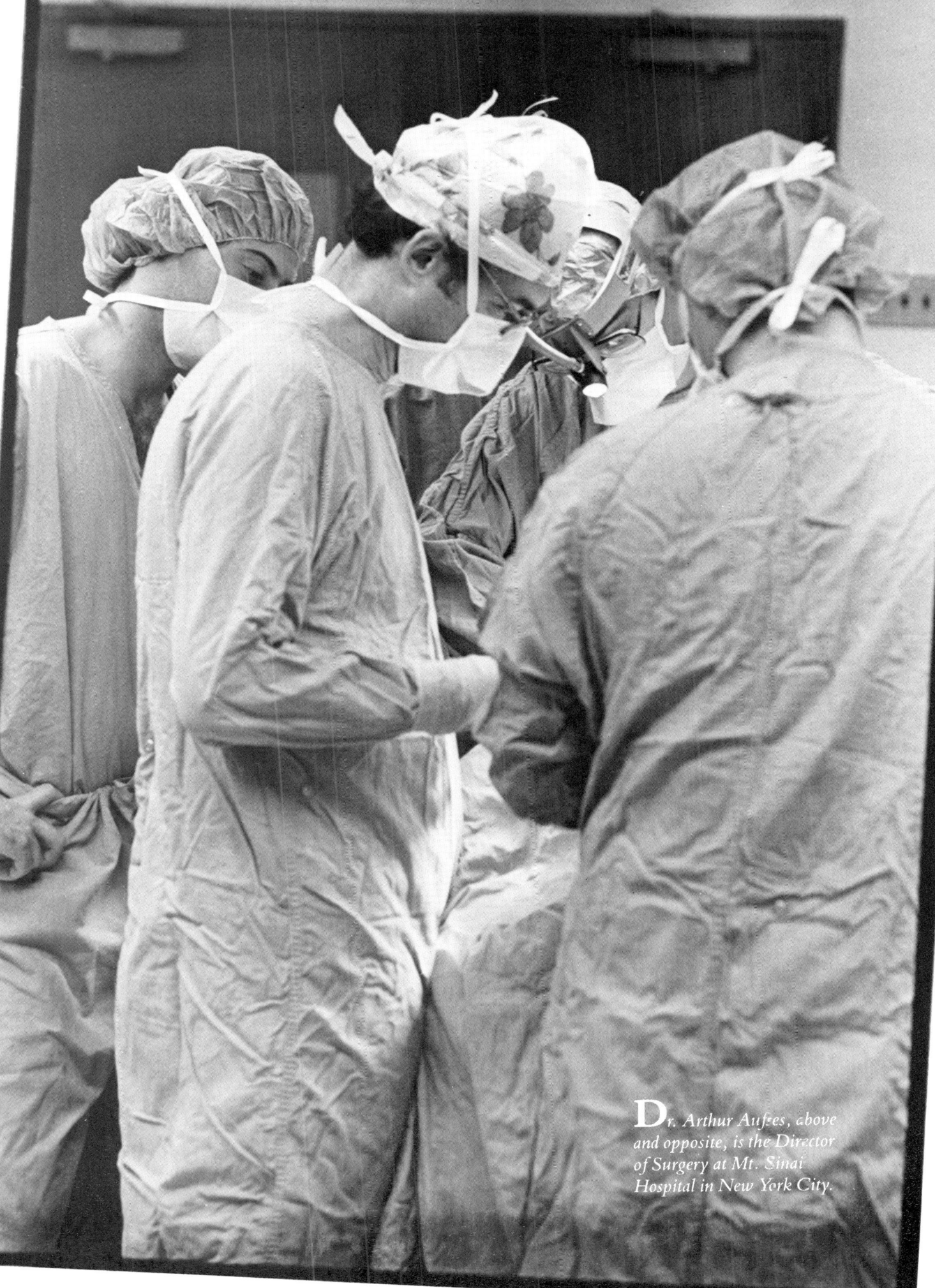

Dr. Arthur Aufses, above and opposite, is the Director of Surgery at Mt. Sinai Hospital in New York City.

torial innovation than except perhaps an apron. Although licensed surgeons began protesting against their ambidextrous counterparts as early as the eighteenth century, barber-surgeons persisted in wielding their razors well into the nineteenth century.

If approached today by a surgeon who was not wearing his or her sterile white coat, cap, and gloves, one would not, we imagine, require the services of the anesthetist. It was not until about one hundred years ago, however, when the theories behind sanitation and infection were finally understood and accepted, that surgeons, legitimate or otherwise, began wearing protective attire.

One of the greatest innovations born of microbiology was the scrub suit. These nonconfining, comfortable outfits are 100% cotton, machine-washable, quick to dry, and shrink- and tear-resistant. Because they don't bind at the knee like garments of heavier materials, they're lots more comfortable for exercising than jeans or regular slacks. Try them as summer pajamas—they're tops for cool comfort.

NURSES

Before Florence Nightingale established her training school for nurses in 1860, the first angels of medical mercy were nuns, and as such, wore the habit determined by their religious order. But with the advances in medicine during the middle part of the nineteenth century, medical uniforms as well as medical practice changed radically.

As one can see, though, from the list of clothes carried to the Crimean War by Ms. Nightingale's army—one gray tweed dress known as a wrapper, one gray worsted jacket, one plain white cap, one short woolen cloak, and one holland scarf—washability was not at first of prime importance. Many of these medical helpmeets even tucked some lovely if unwashable blue serge garments into their portmanteaux. These stalwart missionaries complained of neither the situation nor their "uniforms," but only of the requisite and apparently dreadfully uncomfortable headress: "I came along," pleaded one to her exasperated superior, "prepared to submit to everything... But there are some things, Ma'am, one can't submit to... If I'd known, Ma'am, about the caps, great as my desire... I wouldn't have come."

Although the Red Cross was established by Jean Henri Dunant in Switzerland in the middle of the nineteenth century, it was Clara Barton who, in 1881, incorporated the organization and changed it into one that would serve the world in peace as well as war. By the early twentieth century, members of this world-renowned service organization were known as daughters of the "Greatest Mother in the World."

In 1918, when nurses were required not just to soothe and comfort but "to apply the delicate and continued modern treatments

Below, a contemporary nurses uniform from Bencone. See Index.

"Not a frill that would harbor germs—not a useless button sewn on—nothing to tear easily is permitted," declared the Red Cross Manual in 1918. Nurses had to be ready to work hard—so, too, did their clothing.

Above: An American Red Cross nurse wearing the now-famous red-lined dark blue cape for use in cooler climates.

which save so many lives and prevent innumerable amputations," the uniform changed from the idiosyncratic and on occasion motley one worn by Nightingale's forces and Civil War volunteers to one designed for the nurse's part in "aseptic surgery." "Not a frill that would harbor germs—not a useless button to sew on—nothing to tear easily is permitted. The only additions sanctioned are her treasured military or naval nursing insignia or her Red Cross emblem on her cap, sleeve, or badge."

An American Red Cross nurse heading for the villages of Brittany during the first part of the twentieth century would probably count among her wardrobe:

- a gray cotton crepe working uniform worn while in the fields and known as the "uniform that our wounded know best"
- a boxy and decidedly unromantic utility apron "adopted to simplify the ever present French laundry problem" and worn over the gray uniform while in the operating room
- a white dress uniform considered a "mark of honor—and one which is dramatic in its symbolism," worn during a general's visit or other formal occasion
- a now-famous red-lined dark blue cape most likely worn smartly with the lining thrown over one shoulder
- a gray summer outdoor uniform worn especially by members stationed in Palestine, Greece, Italy, France, England, and the United States, or wherever an "emergency of war" must be met
- rubber boots and a "sou'wester"
- a heavy ulster worn in sleeping tents as well as outdoors (the able-bodied nurses maintained that while wrapped in their ulsters "they were as warm as those within solid walls")

A "town and country" nurse (one assigned to rural communities in North America) might add to this wardrobe a plain blue gingham dress with a soft collar and cuffs, a panama hat, and an emergency kit in which she carried "a new lease of life for all to whom it opens". Recipients of Red Cross aid were to be assured that these new hygienic uniforms in no way made modern nurses any "less sympathetic—less mothering" than their forebears.

Today nurses' uniforms for both women and men are made of affordable and easy-to-care-for cotton or cotton/polyester blends. Elasticized waists, roomy pockets, and no-iron fabrics make these garments perfect for anyone who must put in a long day. If you've got a job that keeps you on your feet most of the day, look into buying a pair of nurse's shoes. These premium-grade leather shoes are constructed with built-in arch supports, ventilated uppers, and slip-resistant soles. Wraparound jackets, worn by nurses, lab technicians, and pharmacists, are perfect for people with young children; the reverse front enables the caretaker to cover the soiled area and look as fresh as he or she did before Junior decided he didn't like the spinach.

Photographer Georgina Bedrosian's eclectic outfit is highlighted by a cool and roomy side buttoning dentist's smock. It's belted over a pair of Japanese baseball pants and British football socks.

Real Clothes 115

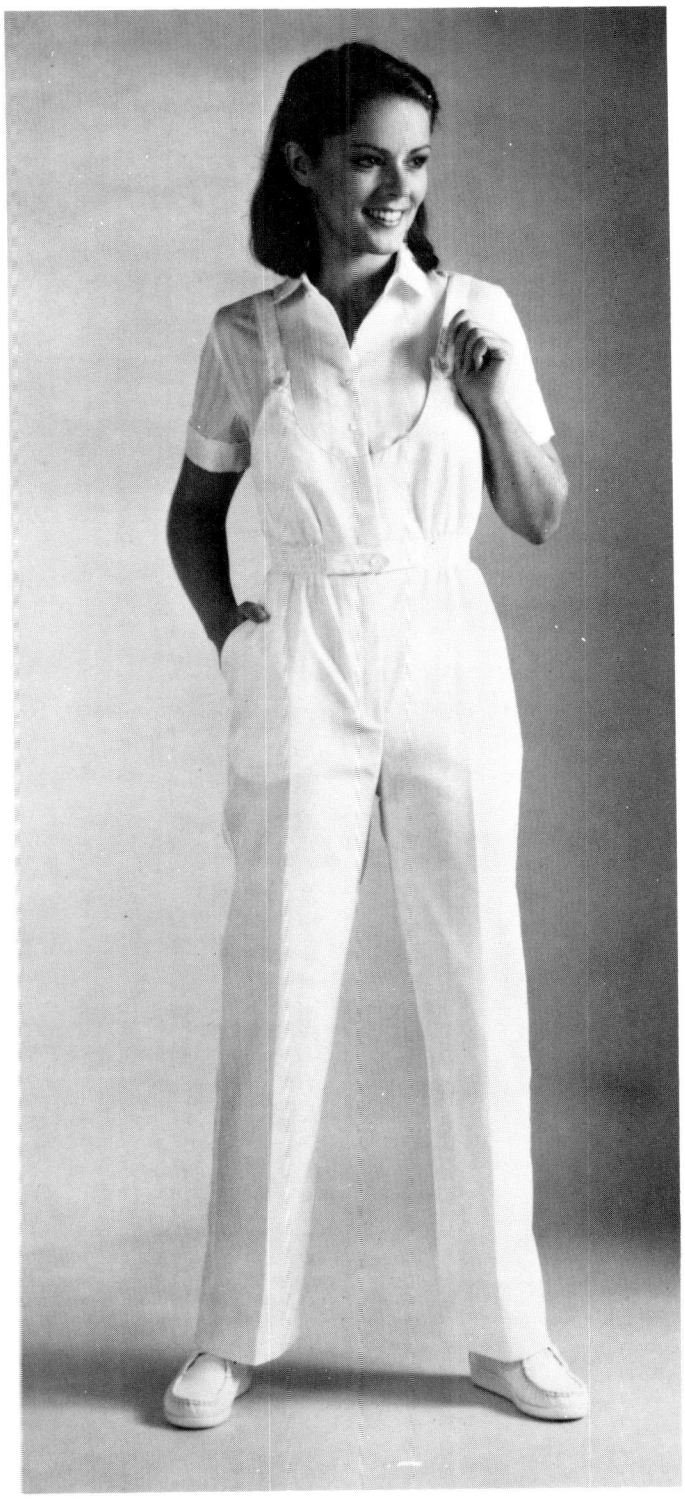

On these two pages, three practical, all white nurse's outfits. Made from a sturdy dacron-cotton blend that takes a beating but comes back as bright-white as ever, these jumpsuits, jumpers, and overalls are neatly tailored, comfortable, and they'll wear forever. All from White Swan (see Index).

116   Real Clothes

More goodies from Bencone. Below, jogging pants and sweatshirts. Right, easily washable nurses's tops—lightweight, comfortable.

Blast out of the past in this rugged air force jumpsuit. It has pockets everywhere, and if that's not enough, add an all leather Swedish Army belt. Both from I. Buss. Model: Maryanne Horwath. Photographed at the Cloisters Cafe, New York City.

7

UNCLE SAM

*guernseys • helmets • combat
boots • document pouches*

In 1941, British Major-General O'Connor stands at the ready in his heavy wool melton coat.

Military uniforms are made to take a tough beating. Unlike department stores, Uncle Sam will only accept goods that meet his rigorous specifications, and that means that only the hardiest of fibers, careful stitching, and topnotch construction will be accepted. Military clothes are also one of the last sources of superior-quality clothes made in pure, natural cotton, wool, and leather. So besides feeling good, these clothes will last forever.

ON THE SEA

There are two principles guiding the design of clothes worn at sea: First, whatever the garment be, it must not hinder the wearer as he or she works the ropes or sails; second, it must protect the sailor against the weather.

In keeping with these principles, the first sailors worked naked (although a coatlike overgarment was dispatched to less hardy mates). When these swarthy explorers reached the northern seas, though, even the most stalwart found himself covered with gooseflesh, and so simple tunics, similar in structure to those worn by farm laborers during the Middle Ages, were worn.

In the sixteenth and seventeenth centuries, when sailors realized they could save their bodies significant wear and tear if they covered their legs,

Besides feeling great to wear, military clothes last forever. And they aren't just oversized olive drab fatigues, either—many jackets, pants, and dresses are elaborately tailored, trim fitting garments.

Maria Miller's all-cotton military "gas coat" liner makes a great artists smock for her office.

many began wearing baggy "canvice" breeches known as "slops" or "slop hose." When coated with tar, slops became a formidable if not particularly malleable garment made of "tarpaulin." In poor weather, short petticoats called "rugges" might be worn over slops. Shoes were almost always double-soled for extra protection.

By the eighteenth century, the well-outfitted sailor wore breeches and a jacket, shirt, and waistcoat. (By the way, contrary to the popularly held notion imposed on the past by our own chauvinistic times, women have always been an active if candestine part of the sailing forces of the world; because they were forced to conceal their gender, their garments exactly imitated men's.) Toward the middle of the century, sailors adopted trousers, the latest fashion innovation. These loose, comfortable garments were worn six inches above the ankle (as sailors well knew, skin dries faster than cloth): by 1817, the first slightly longer and wider "gun-mouthed" or "bell-bottomed" trousers were worn.

Oilskin may well be the innovation that most radically altered the sailor's wardrobe. Legend has it that the invention of oilskin can be attributed to an assiduous sailor who, in searching for a waterproof packing material a few hundred years ago, impregnated scraps of silk, linen, and cotton with boiled linseed oil. During the nineteenth century, this sailor's spiritual descendant discovered that when combined with pipe clay, linseed oil became a more protective and water-repellent material than the stuff his forebear had developed. It didn't take long for sailors to begin making their hats, trousers, jackets, and every other sartorial necessity out of this resilient, water-repellent material.

The now acclaimed jersey, or guernsey, was worn by sailors of the nineteenth century (Lord Nelson wrote about the special advantages of a guernsey jacket as early as 1804). These heavy-duty sweaters (some weigh two pounds!), also called ganseys and ganzeys, are traditionally made in gray or dark blue and provide the ultimate in comfort and style for those on or off the seas.

ON THE LAND

It's hard to imagine, but during the latter part of the eighteenth century, the entire U. S. Army consisted of one infantry regiment. You see, it happened like this: When General Washington put out the call for troops, only two of four states (New Jersey and Pennsylvania, and not Connecticut and New York) saw fit to send men.

The first uniform approved by Washington consisted of a blue coat with a smart-looking red facing. But despite their small numbers, some detachments were unable to provide the money required to buy the fancy red cloth so favored by the general. (It's been said that in an attempt to procure the requisite funds, some less merciful sergeants tried—unsuccessfully—to halt the rum ration.) In actuality, then, the first American army uniform consisted of anything from a European-style full-dress uniform to a blanket with a hole cut in it for the head. Oftentimes, men wore stockings but not shoes, and some donned fashionable top hats and overcoats, but had no shirt to show beneath. If boots were worn, they were most often of the "country" variety; that is, they consisted of scraps of cloth folded around the leg and tied at the knee and ankle like an Indian legging. Many officers, even those in charge of more financially solvent detachments, were reluctant to provide their men with uniforms, for the men, it seems, were somewhat disrespectful of the goods: The "Rogues and whores that went with the baggage" frequently sold or traded their fancily tailored ducs for a pint.

This is not to imply that the army was completely without regulations: It's on record that every enlisted man was required to wash his hands and face once a day.

By 1830, a full-dress uniform elaborate enough to have satisfied even the stylish Washington was adopted. Not a mere twenty-five years later, these highly ornamental outfits, replete with shakos, were refused by the men called to defend the Mexican-American border. Constrained by their heavy, excessively tailored garments, these soldiers found the enemy and the sweltering heat nearly unmasterable foes. By the 1860s, their vociferous protests had altered the basic field-duty uniform into one that was relatively comfortable and free of adornment. Officers, however, continued to wear elegant dress uniforms for ceremonial occasions.

The first khaki tropical service uniform was adopted in the last years of the nineteenth century for use in Cuba, Puerto Rico, and the Philippines. This simply cut and minimally ornamented outfit consisting of breeches and a frocklike coat was worn with leather leggings (canvas for the men of lower rank) and proved one of the most functional uniforms ever made for the force.

It was the American Expeditionary Forces in France who in 1918 wore the first olive drab wool uniform and the steel British-style "basin" helmet. High brown leather boots protected the feet and calves of officers while puttees—cloth strips wrapped around the leg from ankle to knee—were provided for soldiers.

During the Second World War, uniform designers continued to modify the field-duty uniform for better protective coloration and simplicity of style. The olive green uniform for example, worn by enlisted men in 1945, was made of individual pieces that could be adapted to the differing needs of various branches of the service. While in Europe, most combat troops wore wool trousers, a cotton field jacket, a wool scarf, leather gloves, and leather field shoes or laced combat boots. Concealing white covers were worn over helmets in winter, dark green in the summer.

By 1963, new weapons such as the M-14 required new ways of carrying ammunition, and army engineers made uniforms designed

Author Susan Osborn found this sailor's shirt at a secondhand store, and added her own scarf to complete the outfit. It's crisp white cotton— works well on land, too.

Book designer Sasan Wilson likes this heavy cotton-duck sailor's top —actually a contemporary re-creation from Land's End (see Index).

Graphic designer Traci Churchill wearing a jumpsuit reminiscent of that on our opening spread, with a high tech ribbed belt from Charivari, NYC.

When summer rolls around, film maker Fern Galperin pulls out her favorite pair of shorts—authentic British Army shorts of cotton khaki. Front pleated, button fly, and a wrap waist that buckles on both sides. The British first discovered khaki (an ancient Hindu word meaning dusty) in the early 19th century, when they were stationed in India, and it's been used for army uniforms ever since.

with compact and ingenious means of carrying equipment, including all kinds of torso and thigh web straps, hidden pockets, and pouches.

Today, almost any article of military gear can be used as good-looking everyday wear. Try a pair of French Foreign Legion shoes. These sturdy, cotton duck bootlike shoes were originally designed for the jungle, but their superior soles provide great grip on city sidewalks, and in case you get caught in the rain, the hemp insoles are removable and dry quickly. An all-leather document pouch similar to the ones used during the First World War are great for traveling and can be used to hold your passport, hotel keys, traveler's checks, and sunglasses. With its roomy snap-shut pockets, cotton lining, and drawstring waist and bottom, a khaki field jacket remains one of the best-looking and most effective coverups around.

THE SALVATION ARMY

Not really a military organization, this unique army of about 3 million has troops in eighty-six countries who continue to crusade for our salvation. A volunteer organization, originally called the East London Christian Mission, it was founded in 1865 by the Reverend William Booth and his wife Catherine. The Booths felt that their missionaries' uniforms should be designed to coordinate with the crusading spirit of the campaign; thus the red, blue, and yellow color scheme still worn by today's Salvationists symbolizes the blood of Christ, the fire of the Holy Ghost, and the purity of life.

During the first years of their crusade, these determined prohibitionists discovered that they had to find some sort of headgear that would protect them from the arsenal of stones, eggs, and tomatoes cast their way by angry publicans. Many of the men improvised a military-style helmet of any sturdy material available. The women, however, found suitable protection in the wide-brimmed "Hallelujah bonnet" devised by Mrs. Booth (or, as she was known, "our sainted Army mother"). These ordinary black bonnets, trimmed with a plain pleated band of black silk at the base of the crown and decorated with black strings, were disdained by some of the first twenty-five female cadets, who felt they were conspicuously old-fashioned. Mrs. Booth quickly disabused them of this notion. Perhaps in an attempt to symbolize their determination to stand fast against brickbats and missiles, in 1883, the band members began wearing cast-off army uniforms.

While the size of the bonnet brim and the hem of the women's unadorned frock have fluctuated with time, virtually all else about the Salvation Army uniform remains unchanged. If you're lucky enough to find a Salvation Army jacket in a thrift shop, hold on to it. It'll last you for years.

*F*ashion buyer Andy Maag layers a modified bomber jacket/vest over a khaki band collar shirt and a cool gray tee.

Authenic reproductions of World War II sheepskin flight jackets are made from the finest materials available. Exceptionally warm and comfortable, they boast brown leather exteriors and thick sheep fur linings. Quartermaster Uniform Company.

130 Real Clothes

All from Quartermaster: above, Air Force Overseas Flight Cap of texturized polyester. Right, this heavy anodized belt buckle is for wearing with your "dress blues."

Heavyweight adjustable bleached white pistol belts with or without eyelets. Each is 2¼" wide and the one in the center has a brass parade dress buckle.

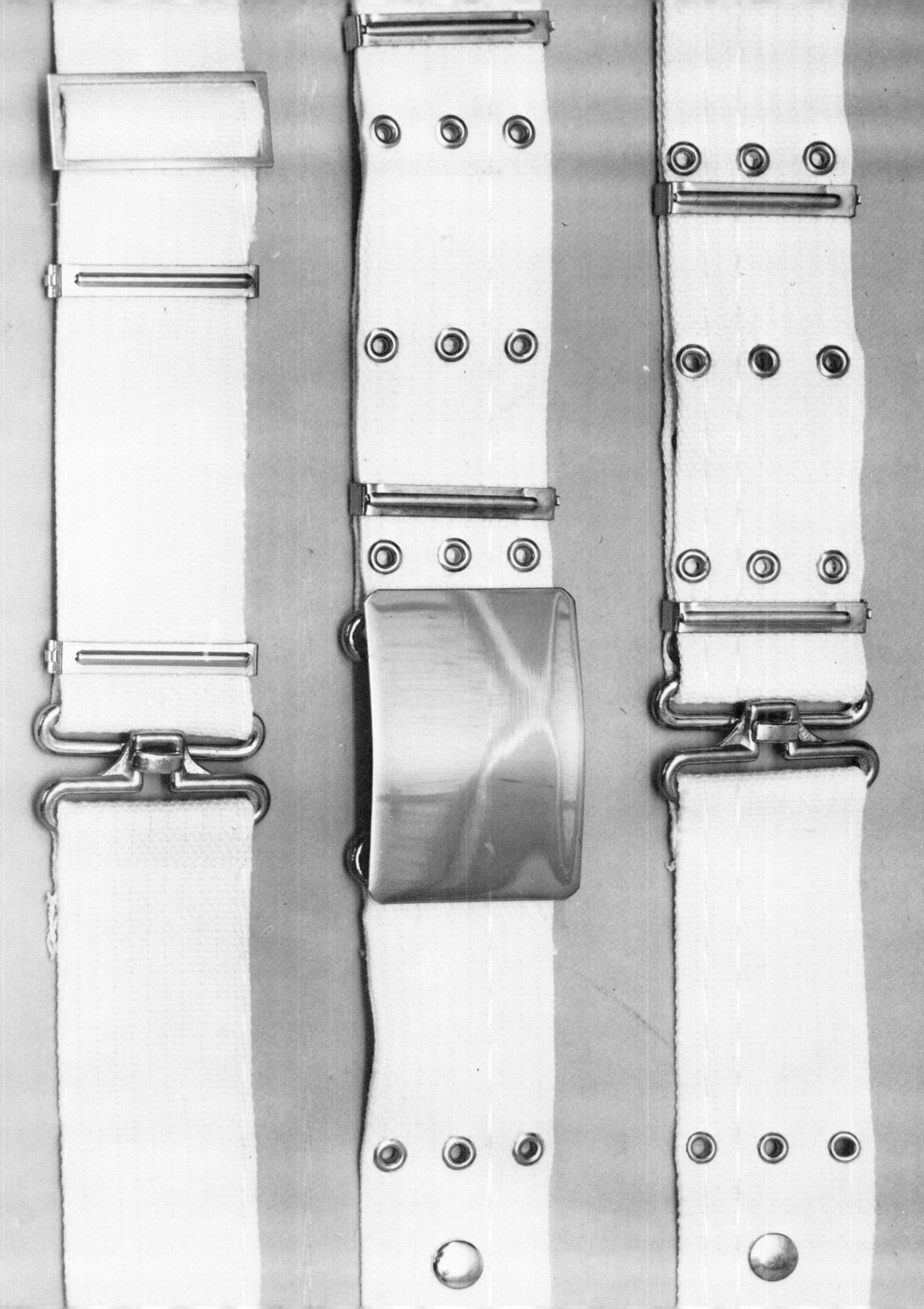

Break away from the herd. Model Giorgio Paulino in a tan cotton duck "duster" on Manhattan's Park Avenue. Kauffman and Sons Saddlery has perpetuated this favored classic from the Old West—designed to protect the rider yet allow him freedom of movement, it features a long center vent, two way pockets, and can be snapped around each leg for riding.

8

COWBOY ELEGANCE

jeans • spurs • chaps • boots • overalls

U ntil recently, equal doses of poverty and humility combined to keep land workers' clothes coarse and free of ornament. These clothes were then and are now designed to survive strenuous activity, and that means hardy fibers, double—if not triple—stitching, and impeccable construction.

COWBOYS

American cowpunchers are descendants of the Spanish-American *vaqueros*, who in turn are cousins of the European Moors. Although jeans are the uniform we associate with cowboys, these practical and long-lasting garments were first disdained by cowboys, who considered them a lower-class innovation. It was at least forty years after Levi Strauss made his first pair of legendary trousers before cowpokes gave them a try.

When Levi Strauss landed in America in 1848, he was carrying a couple of bolts of canvas that he hoped to sell to the rough-and-tumble settlers for tenting. Only problem was, the canvas made a lousy tent. During the course of a conversation in which Strauss bemoaned his plight to a disgruntled miner, the miner mentioned that he was having trouble finding a pair of pants sturdy enough to withstand the rigors of digging. Dauntless Mr. Strauss measured the man on the spot and for six dollars in gold dust sold him the first

B*ottom: the duster as it was advertised in the 1910 Sears Catalog. Opposite: As far back as 1915, cowboy clothing suggested rugged elegance.*

pair of Levi's. The rest, as they say, is history.

Today, jeans (the word is derived from Gênes, the French word for Genoa, where a cloth similar to the serge de Nîmes denim, originally used by Strauss is made) are available prewashed, preshrunk, and prefaded, and are easily adapted to any fashion idiosyncrasy: Women can transform them into skirts, men can use them as swim trunks. And Strauss's distinguished trousers are still making history: It was only recently reported that a construction worker dangled fifty-two stories above the street supported only by a rope hooked through the belt loop of his Levi's.

When riding, cowpokes often wore chaps (known to the poetic among them as "shotguns"). These stiff, tight cowhide panels looked manly and were eminently practical, particularly the batwing type that allowed riders great freedom of movement as they protected their legs and trousers. Today, chaps are made in leather and suede or even in bear, wolf, pony, sheep, or angora fur and can be zipped over anyone's trousers for a unique, rugged look.

Like the other parts of the outfit, a cowboy's shirt was designed to satisfy the rigorous requirements of the job. The broad shoulders allow freedom of action when riding and roping, the tapered body minimizes the amount of fabric that might catch on a steer horn, and the yoke adds an extra layer of fabric against the cold. Vests were commonly worn over the shirt and provided cowboys with a symbolic link between the world of the range and the world of business.

Hats not only provided range riders with comfortable protection against the sun and rain, but were also employed as pillows, signal flags, bellows, whips, and drinking cups (for horse and rider). Today, as before, tall crowns and wide brims are the favored protection against the sun of the Southwest; lower crowns and narrower brims are preferred to ward off the cold of the Great Plains and Rocky Mountains. The Stetson—*a.k.a.* the "Boss of the Plains"—created not on the range but in the back room of a shop in Philadelphia by an urbanite with a good imagination named Stetson, remains one of the most popular hats available.

The low, embossed purple lizard or red calf cowboy boots sold in today's department stores would hardly be recognized by real cowpokes or frontiersmen. Real cowboy boots are tall and strictly functional, designed to protect the rider's toes and shins from the hazards of ranch work. The thin, tapered toe makes finding the stirrup that much easier, and the top is stitched to prevent chafing. The best boots have a steel shank and wooden peg within to ensure arch support. When buying, look for a leather lining—since synthetic liners do not expand or contract at the same rate as the outside leather, they will gradually separate from the boot. Because cowboy boots are not designed to hug the heel, you should expect a certain slippage when you first put them on. If you don't

feel it, the boot is either too short or too tight.

The once requisite spurs, no longer the malicious sharp metal "prickes" they were during the Middle Ages, are available blunt- or rowel-ended, and although urban cowboys don't need them, they do add an unforgettable touch of class.

Anyone looking for cowboy fashion shouldn't miss real cowboy gloves. Originally made to protect hands from rope burns, these elegant buckskin gloves are available with flared gauntlet wrists and decorated with anything from plastic beads to rhinestones. If you can find some with leather cuff guards, all the better.

FARMERS

Unlike cowboys, the first farmers did everything they could to transform their sackcloths of hodden gray into a merrier kind of garment. In fact, during the Middle Ages, it was not uncommon for field laborers to bedeck themselves with fine colors, pointed shoes, and tight doublets with ornamental buttons. Chaucer reported that some even combed their hair so that it "strouted as a fanne, large and brode." By the fifteenth century, those who could donned parti-colored hose under their tunics.

Of course, those without an extra farthing or two sported naught but a shirt and soled hose in the summer, and a coarse cloak filled with holes in the winter.

By the sixteenth century, both rural and urban residents were beginning to recognize the prophylactic benefits of full-length leg coverings. Laborers eschewed the fashionable trunk hose, though, for they found both the exaggerated "upper stock" and the tight "nether stock" of those bulbous-topped tights impractical. Instead, they opted for separate breeches and stockings. (It was not only laborers who found these wide-thighed breeches inconvenient. In 1592, trunk hose were stuffed so full "with woods, with flaxe, with hair," even "with cattell's tails," that the British Parliament ordered a separate gallery built to accommodate those members who wore them.)

Trunk hose assumed a more natural shape during the seventeenth and eighteenth centuries, and these were worn by laborers under a smock usually crafted from a sack with a hole cut for the head (in *Under the Greenwood Tree*, Hardy describes Thomas Leaf wearing a "long white smock of pillow-case cut"). Because these smocks hang straight down from the body, shed rain, and are relatively windproof, they are ideal for outdoor workers or anyone who wants good-looking, long-lasting protection against the elements. If you buy a smock, look for those evolved from the original Welsh fisher's smock. These fully cut wool flannel or cotton moleskin overshirts sport a high, wide stand-up collar that slips easily over the head and convenient three-quarter-length sleeves. These handsome and utilitarian overshirts can be used at

Carpenter Bud Jantz-Sell and his son Chris know what to wear when they have a job to do — sturdy denims.

Work boots will take a beating. You'll probably wear out before the shoes do.

home, in the office, or during recreational activities, and because they're made of such hardy fabrics, they'll maintain their smart appearance even after hundreds of machine washings.

Not surprisingly, clothes designed for female field laborers were much slower to change than men's. During the Middle Ages, a one-piece, floor-length gown called a kirtle was worn with a wide-sleeved overgarment on top. This impractical covering made gleaning an even more odious chore, for the loose, wide sleeves had to be tied behind the back so they would not interfere with the work. Until the eighteenth century, poverty was the only permissible excuse for a shorter-than-ankle-length skirt, and until the early twentieth century, most women workers were required to wear some kind of headdress, regardless of the weather.

By the sixteenth and seventeenth centuries, the kirtle evolved into a long skirt that was comfortably worn—relatively speaking—with a separate bodice. Feet were covered with practical if precarious pattens, those little wooden-soled shoes with metal rings strapped to the soles to keep toes from being muddied.

It was only during the eighteenth century that a few brave female farm laborers wore ingeniously devised "pants." By pinning their long skirts in the shape of pants and hitching them up to the knees, these women were allowed much more freedom of motion than their forebears. By the end of the nineteenth century, some "eccentrics" were permitted rational clothes like bloomers; other pioneers borrowed their husbands' trousers.

Today both female and male field workers are more likely than not wearing overalls. This trusted garment, once not illogically referred to as "overhauls," was originally an apron, but with the advent of machinery in the nineteenth century, manufacturers attached both trousers and a bib to ensure greater protected against the capriciousness of machines. In the late 1800s, farmers discovered that the garment made a handy cover-up when worn over pants and shirts in the winter, and when worn alone, overalls become the perfect all-purpose work uniform for the summer. The "American-style" overalls with the patent brace fasteners were first introduced in 1905, and they remain one of the most comfortable and long-lasting garments available today.

Rick Hine's Orange, Connecticut, dairy farm has been in his family since 1639, long before "American style" overalls were invented in 1905. He knows what to wear for pure practicality, function, and—not least—comfort. These well broken-in overalls are by Carters, boots by Knapp, hat by Milk Flo.

140 Real Clothes

Left: you'll be sure to get compliments when you don the pin check shirt in blue with dark blue yoke, "smile" pockets, pearl snaps. Right: a classic gingham shirt—back to basics with the timeless styling of red or blue checks on white, accented with flap breast pockets and highlighted with pearl snaps on the cuffs, pockets, front. From Kauffman's.

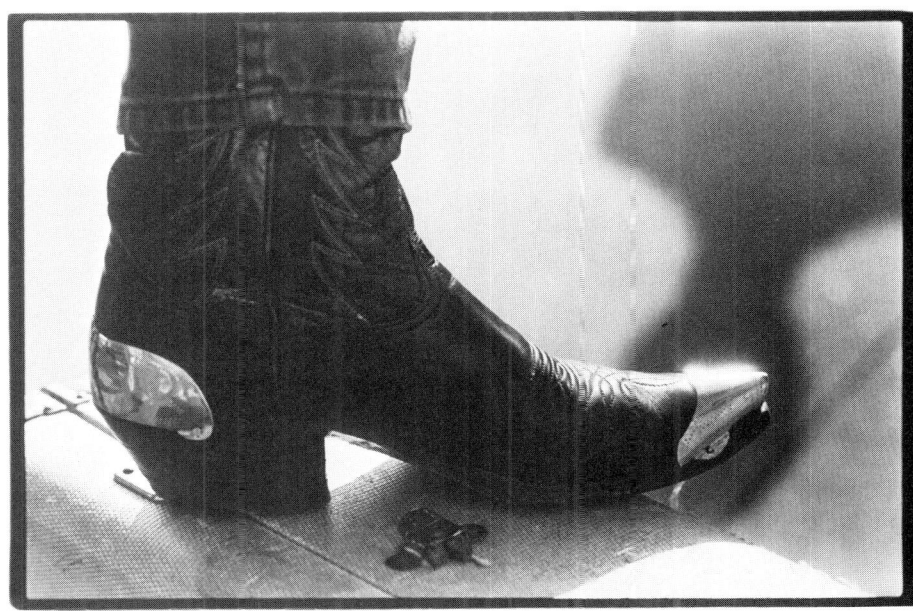

East Village film maker Kevin Downs, rockabilly style. His blue jean vest is accessorized with brass collar tips uncovered at a flea market—they screw on and come right off for laundering. The belt is available from many Western suppliers, and the boot tips and heel "scallops" which brighten Kevin's boots come from Kauffman and Sons. Photographed on The Bowery in New York City.

Left: a hooded riding tunic of waterproof olive nylon with a bright yellow slicker lining and drawstring hood is fully reversible. Lightweight, 50" x 80". Center, the Kauffman Duster, also featured on our opening spread—great on and off the horse. Right, the saddle slicker is designed to protect you and the saddle from the elements. Bright yellow vinyl. All from Kauffman's.

Twenty pearled snaps give this bib front shirt, in red or blue denim, a rugged by decidedly stylish profile. Western shirts traditionally have snaps instead of buttons—snaps released more easily if a cowboy "caught a horn."

Room to move—and plenty of it in these railroad baggage handler's baggy clothes.

REAL CLOTHES

THE BEST CATALOGS

ALL CITIES UNIFORM COMPANY
Police and Fire Department uniforms and equipment. Great "wool blouses" that look as sharp as blazers, with only half the weight.
*992-4 Madison Avenue
Paterson, NJ 07501
201 742-9684*

AMERICAN WORKING WOMEN'S SUPPLY COMPANY
Rosie-the-Riveter would have cheered this collection of work gloves and boots that are built for comfort and all-out durability—but sized for smaller hands and feet. Looks that say STRONG—with style! To send for: *Blue Collar Jobs for Women*, by Muriel Lederer—a comprehensive guide to 80 of the best—how they pay, what's in it for you, how to get started.

*P.O. Box 100
Deer Park, New York 11729
516 667-6266*

ANARTEX LTD. SHEEPSKINS
Classic sheepskin coats and jackets in more styles than there are states in the union. Don't miss it.

*Lomond Industrial Estate
Alexandria, Dunbartonshire
SCOTLAND*

ANTLER
Industrial & Uniform Outerwear; hunting and insulated apparel. Rugged stuff. For the Marlboro Man in your life. A Division of M. Rubin & Sons, Inc.
*10 W. 33rd St.
New York, N.Y. 10001
212 431-5400*

ARMY & NAVY SUPPLY STORE
By now we are all familiar with Fashions in Fatigues, no?—But don't forget about all the basics in camping equipment and—who knows—we may all need these people to dispense gas masks to the civilian population someday. But don't bother with any of this if olive drab just isn't your color.
*1938 3rd Avenue
New York, N.Y. 10029
212 534-1600*

ASIAN MARTIAL ARTS SUPPLIES
We wonder if Bruce Lee had a supplier this complete. They feature Kung-Fu and karate uniforms and exercise equipment. Chop chop.

*219-10 So. Conduit Ave.
Springfield Gardens, NY 11413
212 978-9797*

BANANA REPUBLIC
Safari and travel clothing. No-nonsense natural fabrics for south of the border. A nifty little catalog that, page for page, is one of the best we've seen. These folks scoured the globe for these items, and it shows.

*PO Box 77133
San Francisco, CA 94107
415 777-5200*

EDDIE BAUER
That Grandaddy of the mail order biz. No-frills outdoor wear for very reasonable prices. A company you can depend on.
*P.O. Box 3700
5th And Union
Seattle, WA 98124
800-426-8020
206 885-3330 (WA)*

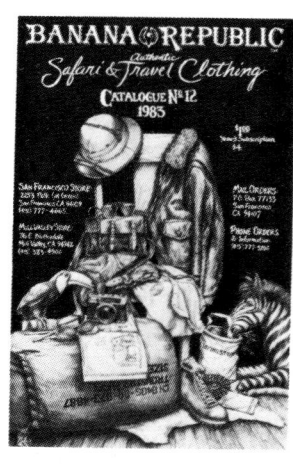

Real Clothes 147

L.L. BEAN
What can we say that you don't already know? To refresh your memory: Chamois cloth shirts, The Gumshoe, All-cotton turtlenecks, shetland Fair-Isle sweaters, flannel pj's . . . ring any bells?
Freeport, ME 04033
204-865-3111

BENCONE UNIFORMS
Large selection of ladies' and men's medical uniforms and shoes at hard to beat prices.
Westwood, NJ 07675
800 631-4602
201 666-4210 (NJ)

THE BEST CHOICE
An "anthology" of name-brand sportswear catalogs: running gear from New Balance, Nike, Sub-4, Adidas; tennis togs from Head, Patagonia and Adidas. Orders shipped within 48 hours. Short and sweet.
253 W. Chocolate Avenue
Hershey, Pennsylvania
800 233-2175 (orders only)
717 533-8339 (info)

BEST UNIFORM COMPANY INC.
More for the Boys in Blue. A classic selection of well-tailored jodphur pants, bloused-back jackets & shirts with McClelland collars.
18 West 18th St.
New York, N.Y. 10011
212 242-4321

BIKE THREADS
The home-spun approach to mail-order. This small, typewritten catalogue contains detailed descriptions of their selections instead of photos or drawings. Many of the prices are handwritten, and the owner's personal signature appears beneath the statement of his sales philosophy. Includes a color insert of Protogs brand sportswear for running, cycling and skating. A company devoted to value.
9434 Beverly Street
Bellflower, California 90706
213 925-2646

BIKECOLOGY INC.
No-nonsense newsprint catalogue for people who'd rather spend their time taking to the road than thumbing through a full-color catalogue.
1515 Wilshire Blvd.
Santa Monica, California 90403
213 394-7059

BILL TOSETTI'S THE PENDLETON SPECIALISTS
Investment dressing: men's and women's separates in Pendleton plaids will never go out of style. Also—ties, mufflers and sports caps that no self-respecting man-about-town should be without. Check out park blankets in bold stripes.
17632 Chatsworth Street
Granada Hills, California 91344
213 363-2192

BLAUER UNIFORM RAINWEAR & OUTERWEAR
Lightweight police and military rainwear that's available in assorted colors. How 'bout men's and ladies' swimwear in high-visibility fluorescent orange for those who like to stand out in the crowd?
160 N. Washington St.
Boston, MA 02114
617 227-1300

BOY SCOUTS OF AMERICA
The official Cub Scout Canteen. The Boy Scout Cook Kit. The Official Scout Pocketknife. It's all here—uniforms, pins, scarves, leadership manuals, and project ideas for kids of all ages. As American and Rin-Tin-Tin.

P.O. Box 175
Bellwood, Illinois 60104
800 323-0732
312 681-6100 (IL)

MOSS BROWN & CO.
In a word: FitnessCenter. Record your progress with their Runners Log—52 weeks of entries. Go for it!

1522 Wisconsin Ave. NW
Washington, DC 20007
800 424-2774

BURKE'S
More and more camping gear. Six pages of backpacks alone, to give you some idea. Also—books! —250 titles on different aspects of outdoor living. No kidding.

7 Bluff Point Road
Northport, N.Y. 11768

I. BUSS & COMPANY
Army Navy rank and file surplus and reproductions: British Navy shorts, jungle fatigues, a great French sailor's dress, drill pants, and more.

738 Broadway
New York, NY 10003
212 242-3338

CAPEZIO BALLET MAKERS
Toe shoes on up, Capezio's has it, and they have since 1887. Not just ballet wear—exercise clothing, tap shoes, t-shirts... a beautiful catalog packed with behind the scenes glimpses of the dance world. Catalog is 3 dollars.

1860 Broadway
New York, New York 10023

CARDINAL INDUSTRIES
Advertising specialty items: caps, jackets, headgear, jumpsuits, totes, bumper stickers, signs and accessories–slick! Both stock and custom emblems available. Be a walking billboard.

Highway 83-689
Box 1430
Grundy, Virginia 24614
800 336-0551
703 935-4845 (VA)

CASCO BAY TRADING POST
Classics for coast and country living. Terrific selection of warm, functional leather gloves. A treat for nimble fingers whose job it is to fetch the fire wood all winter.

Freeport, ME 04032
207 865-6371

CHEERLEADER SUPPLY COMPANY
A far cry from the pom-poms and megaphones of yesteryear. The one-stop shop for Ra-Ra.

Box 80175
Dallas, TX 75230
800-527-4366

COLUMBIA SPORTSWEAR
If you've ever been cold or wet or—(God forbid) both—you won't want to pass up these Hi-tech vests, windshirts and parkas. All in styles and colors that take you from city to country.

P.O. Box 03239
6600 N. Baltimore
Portland, Oregon 97203
503 286-3676

Real Clothes 149

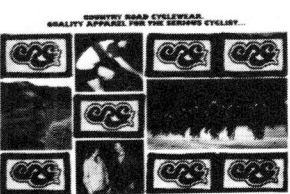

COMMODORE NAUTICAL SUPPLIES
1st class embroidered insignias, emblems & patches. Everything you need to keep your yacht & crew in ship-shape.
396 Broadway, 5th Floor
New York, N.Y. 10013
800-221-7605
212 226-1880 (NY)

COUNTRY ROAD CYCLEWEAR
True, there's a limited selection, but every one a scene-stealer! Polos in tri-color cotton, wool blends, solid cottons —with pockets, pockets everywhere. Break away and send for one!
350 Tower Hill Circle
Golden, CO 80401
303 526-1873

CUTTER BILL WESTERN WORLD
The best that Texas has to offer. Silver belt buckles and hat bands, ladies' prairie skirts, Texas style chili and pralines for Christmas giving plus... top o' the line boots that cost a month's rent. If ya got it, podner, flaunt it.
5818 LBJ Freeway
Dallas, Texas 75240
214 980-4244

DEERSKIN TRADING POST
You must know someone who owns one of those rugged looking sheepskin lined suede jackets. Chances are they got it here.
119 Foster Street, Box 6036
Peabody, MA 01960
617 532-2810

DOLAN'S SPORTS
Martial arts supplies. Next time someone kicks sand in your face, send for this catalog. Pro karate uniforms, all cotton, white or black, are among the few items that don't take special training to handle.
PO Box 26
Farmingdale, New Jersey 07727
201 938-6656

DORNAN UNIFORMS
A Small company specializing in classy uniforms for household staffs. Treat your chauffeur to a pair of dashing patent porvair oxfords.
653 11th Avenue
New York, NY 10036
212 247-0937
800-223-0363

DUNN's INC.
THE shop for sharpshooters. Hunting and rifling accessories for people who know what they're doing. Strong on leather goods: gun cases, saddles and saddle bags and the best-looking dog collars we've seen yet. Would you believe... Phona-duck... it quacks instead of ringing!
Highway 57E
P.O. Box 449
Grand Junction, Tennessee 38039
901 764-6901

EARLY WINTERS
For people who only come indoors to water the plants: equip yourself to stay warm, stay dry, stay cool, stay quick, stay light—but don't stay off your feet!
110 Prefontaine Place South
Seattle, WA 98104-9977
206 624-5599

EASTERN MOUNTAIN SPORTS
Not just outdoor wear; also includes a complete line of ski, mountain climbing and camping

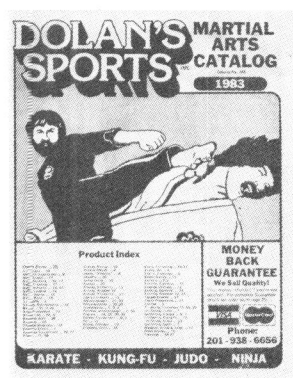

A *warm practical sweater-vest from Wasco.*

Real Clothes 151

equipment. How 'bout a backpack for pooch?
*One Vose Farm Road
Peterborough, NH 03458
603 924-9571*

EASTERN WEAR GUARD
Nifty go-anywhere-do-anything jumpsuits plus work boots that look like they'll last forever. Industrial workclothes, heavy weather gear. Not for city slickers.
*P.O. Box 400
Hingham, MA 02043
800 343-4406*

JAMES G. FAST COMPANY UNIFORMS
First Aid for medical apparel. Stylish designs for women of all shapes and sizes.
*Conway Sports Center
Box 7000
Conway AR 72032
800-643-8378*

FRENCH CREEK SHEEP & WOOL CO.
High quality leather & woolen goods with a country feeling. It ain't cheap, but then neither is the merchandise.
*Elverson, PA 19520
215 286-5700*

FROSTLINE KITS
A great-looking collection of insulated coat, parka and skiwear kits to sew yourself. All kits come ready to sew, at prices that are worth their weight in goose feathers. Spend the money you save on your lift ticket!
*Frostline Circle
Denver, Colorado 80241
303 451-5600*

FUN-WEAR
Lotsa Levi's . . . plus Western wear for the whole family. Good selection of Indian Moccasins, Western boots at reasonable prices and hats to top it off.
*P.O. Box 2800
141 East Elkhorn Avenue
Estes Park, Colorado 80517
303 586-3361*

GAYER'S SADDLERY
You guessed it. Eastern-style tack and accessories for the horse in your life. Limited selection, though.
*6611 Dower House Road
Upper Marlboro, Maryland 20772
301 599-6507*

GOKEY'S
If you've never seen this catalogue, well, you should be ashamed of yourself. What sets Gokey's apart from all the rest is their unbeatable combination of quality workmanship and competitive prices. Top picks: leather oxfords & moccasins that last a lifetime and first-rate leather and canvas duck luggage that looks like a million bucks. The genuine article.
*84 S. Wabasha Street
St. Paul, Minnesota 55107
800 328-9374
612 224-4432 (MN)*

HILL'S COURT
At least you can *look* like a pro. Also—sweats of all colors and descriptions, aerobic paraphernalia, poolside accessories.
*Manchester, VT 05254
802 362-1200*

HUDSON'S
How about: French sailing shirts, sweat shirts, chambray shirts, tennis shirts, running shirts, rugby shirts, canvas shirts? And that's only the shirts! Shorts, too,

and pants, shoes, jackets for outdoors, sports, camping. And belts, and . . .

97 Third Avenue
New York, NY 10003
212 598-0020

H. KAUFFMAN & SONS SADDLERY

A wonderful catalog stocked chock full with American and English riding gear and accessories for you and your mount.

141 East 24th Street
New York, NY 10010
(212) 684-6060

KANDEL KNITS INC.

Terrifically tailored cheerleading outfits for men and women in colors like Scarlet or Kelly . . . and some of the designs are frankly innovative. Most of the sweaters—striped, v'd, buttoned, and hooded —are definitely worth a look.

4834 N. Interstate Avenue
Portland, Oregon 97217
phone not listed

KREEGER & SONS

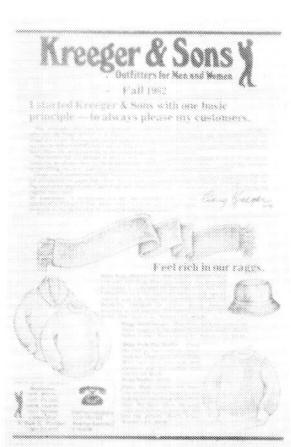

Pants like Mom bought you. Pure silk long johns. Goosedown outerwear. Nifty soft luggage. Chamois Cloth bathrobe –luxurious! And a guarantee that puts your money where their mouth is. It's the American way.

Outfitters for the Outdoors
16 West 46th Street
New York, New York 10036
212 575-7825

LAND'S END DIRECT MERCHANTS

State-of-the-art in mail-order merchandise. Chesapeake-chic forever.

Land's End Lane
Dodgeville, WI 53533
800 356-4444
608 935-2788 (WI)

LIBERTYVILLE SADDLE SHOP

Put your horse on the best dressed list. Incredible selection of English and Western tack from all over the world. You just won't believe all the stuff they've got in this catalogue.

306 Peterson Road
P.O. Box M
Libertyville, Illinois 60048
312 362-0570

MAGSON UNIFORMS

A wide selection of men's and ladies leather jackets and parkas that made us snap-to attention. Get your handcuffs here.

279 New Britain Road
Kensington, CT 06037
203 225-8651

MAJOR LEAGUE BASEBALL RETAIL CATALOG

Much more than the usual fare. Everything from shoelaces and children's playwear to gumball banks and thermal mugs. Top notch. For more information on licensed manufacturers and outlets, write to:

Major League Baseball Promotion Corporation
1212 Avenue of the Americas
New York, N.Y. 10036
212 921-8100

MELCO, INC.

High tech disposable clothing that you won't want to throw away. Made from a tough "miracle material"—jumpsuits, shirts, coveralls, labcoats. Incredibly inexpensive.

6603D Governor Printz Boulevard
Wilmington, DE 19809
800 441-9749

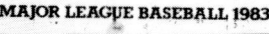

Real Clothes 153

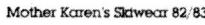

MIDWESTERN DEERWEAR

Davy Crockett was here. Wide selection of genuine deerskin coats, jackets, gloves, wallets and purses. Prices are only listed in the back of the catalogue —a pain, but probably worth the effort.

Berlin, Wisconsin 54923
414 361-2555

MILLER'S

The Tiffany's of the equestrian set. Includes a complete line of English riding attire & tack plus hundreds of can't-live-without items for horsey. Good selection of leather gloves at very reasonable prices. Not for Cowboys.

235 Murray Hill Parkway
East Rutherford, NJ 07073
Retail:
123 E. 24th St.
New York, NY 10010
212 673-1400

MOTHER KAREN'S SKI & SPORTSWEAR

Mother Karen must have been a downhill racer. These skiwear selections were designed by someone who knew what she was doing! Catalogue also includes detailed info on all fabrics used to help make sure that your selection is the right one for you. See also Mother Karen's catalogue for summer sportswear selections. Thanks, Mom!

3479 SW Temple
Salt Lake City, Utah 84115

NASSAU SKATE SHOP

Complete ice-skating outfitters. Including the line of Tai & Randy bodywear by Polar Sport. An Olympic contender.

Nassau County Arena
Magnolia Blvd. and Bay Drive
Long Beach, New York 11561
516 889-3838

NEW ENGLAND DIVERS

For our web-footed friends, a complete line of diving gear and accessories, from the basic amateur wet suit, flippers and snorkel to the most sophisticated commercial jetsuits and compressors.

Mail Order Division
1313 Rantoul Street
Beverly, Massachusetts 01915
800 343-8122

THE NFL MERCHANDISE CATALOG

Sporting goods, outdoor wear & accessories to please fans of all ages and gender. Even quilted bedspreads. For more information on licensed distributors, contact:

National Football League Properties
410 Park Avenue
New York, NY 10022
212 838 0660

THE NORTH FACE

Hit the slopes in pared-down ski wear that won't cramp your style. One of our favorites is the Polar-fleece parka—it's like wearing your favorite blanket. Cool colors, too.

999 Harrison Street
Berkeley, CA 94710
1-800-227-2897

THE OFFICIAL NBA MERCHANDISE CATALOG

Note to be missed: Ladies' team jackets in rabbit fur plus the best-looking bath towels in the sports community. Also plenty of the usual team paraphernalia. For more information on licensed distributors, contact:

NBA Properties
645 Fifth Avenue
Olympic Tower
New York, N.Y. 10022
212 826-7000

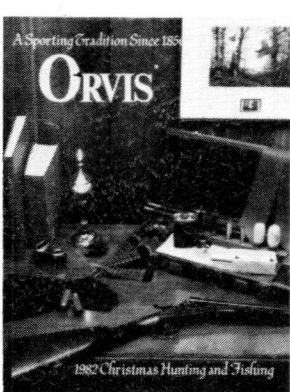

OFFICIAL NEW YORK YANKEE MERCHANDISE

The usual T-shirts, sweatshirts, nightshirts and caps—at better prices than you'd find at the LaGuardia Airport gift shop.

1608 Niagara Falls Blvd.
Tonawanda, New York 14150
phone not listed

OK UNIFORM COMPANY INC.

Shopcoats & overalls. Custom-imprinted t-shirts also available.

512 Broadway
New York, N.Y. 10012
212 966-4733

ORVIS

For the sporting life, it's an American Tradition. Check out the Norfolk shooting coat for your Lord of the Manor. How about a duck-plucker for the man who has everything?

Manchester, Vermont 05254
802 362-1300

P&S OUTDOOR EQUIPMENT AND SUPPLIES

The indispensable field guide to Macho. Even if you're not the King (or Queen) of the Jungle, these classics in camouflage would be a welcome addition to any wardrobe. Not to be missed—the Battle Axe (!) and Ceremonial Saber section.

PO Box 1500
Chapel Hill, NC 27514
800-334-5476
919 929-2183 (NC)

PATAGONIA

Includes photos & testimonials by Real People in Action who've really put Patagonia outerwear to the test. Very convincing. Specializing in highly functional "pile" garments that are lightweight, durable, and insulated against even severest weather conditions. Shop here before your next dog sled race across Alaska.

PO Box 150
Ventura, CA 93002
805 643-8616

PEDAL PUSHER SKI AND SPORT

The Real Good Idea award goes to this catalogue for mercifully supplying its customer with size and color *availability* with pricing on all skis and bindings, boots, etc. They also tell you something about the performance of each series.

445-57 Easton Road
Horsham, Pennsylvania 19044
800 523–7576 (orders)
215 672-0202 (info)

PEDAL PUSHERS

Different spokes for different folks. Frames, wheels, brakes, gears, rims, tubes, clips, caps, shoes, gloves, shorts, seats, books, tools, racks ... Whew! Check it out and go for a ride.

Bicycle specialists
1130 Rogero Road
Jacksonville, Florida 32211
800 874-1736
800 342-7320 (FL)

THE PERFORMANCE BICYCLE SHOP

This is the place to go if you have a hankering to give your bike the works this spring ... by mail! Everything you ever wanted to know about cycling but were afraid to ask.

PO Box 2741
Chapel Hill, NC 27514
800 334-5471

S tyle-wise, not a lot has changed in polo player's clothes since H. Kauffman & Sons ran this photo in a 1930's catalog.

Real Clothes 157

RECREATIONAL EQUIPMENT INC.
A co-op enterprise that seems impressively service oriented. Members are treated to postage-paid orders, toll-free phone line and updates on environmental and expedition support. A catalogue crammed with goodies for life in the great outdoors: from sportswear, luggage and camping equipment to running, mountain climbing and biking gear. A good deal. For more information, contact:

P.O. Box c-88125
Seattle, Washington 98188
800 426-4840
800 562-4894 (WA)

RUSSELL UNIFORM COMPANY
More police and fire garb. Hats off to the firemen's double-breasted overcoats & pea jackets.

44 East 20th St.
New York, NY 10003
212 674-1400

SHEPLER'S
How to look like a Lone-Star native in 10 easy steps. Men's and Ladies' western-style sportswear; boots, belts & buckles galore. For Urban Cowboys: customized accessories for your car or truck. Happy trails.
PO Box 7702
Witchita, KS 67277
800 835-4004

SIERRA DESIGNS
More great-looking parkas and outerwear, with emphasis this time on mountain living. The difference here: detailed info on sleeping bag and tent technology—all about zippers and insulation, care and cleaning, fabric and craftsmanship. Find out what's in it for you.

247 Fourth Street
Oakland, California 94607
For dealer information:
800 227-1097
415 835-4950 (CA)

THE SKIERS' WANTBOOK
That it is. This collection of young, upbeat ski-wear and equipment will take you sailing through the powder in high style. Go for the burn.

307 West 200 South
Suite 5001
Salt Lake City, Utah 84101
800 672-5495
363-8683 (UT)

SPORTS NASHBAR
A to-the-point newsprint catalogue crammed to the gills with ski equipment, racquet sports paraphernalia, shoes and boots. Turn the catalogue around, start from the back and—Presto! You have the Bike Nashbar catalogue. And it contains even more.

215 Main Street
Box 290
New Middletown, Ohio 44442
800 321-2474
216 542-3671

SUB-4 RUNNING APPAREL
As in a sub-4-minute mile. Streamlined warm-ups, track garb and accessories for those who like life in the fast lane.

11615 Coley River Circle
Fountain Valley, CA 92708
800 854-3475
714 754-0491 (CA)

TAFFY'S DANCEWAR
You won't find many tutu's here—their warm ups, leotards, cover ups, aerobic gear & footwear look great *anywhere*. There's something here for any & everyone who

MOVES—and that means YOU.
*701 Beta Drive
Cleveland, OH 44143
216 461 3360*

UNIFORM AND INSIGNIA

Military-mania. It's all here—and we do mean all: Camouflage, dress uniforms, outerwear, fatigues, gym gear, even civil war cavalry hats.

*750 Long Beach Blvd.
Long Beach, CA 90801
213 436-6245*

UNIFORMS, INC.

Specializing in security and protective wear. Great-looking heavy duty coats and jackets.

*2889 W. Olympic Blvd.
Los Angeles, CA 90006
213 383-1395*

WASCO SPORTS, INC.

Distributors of Colmar Italian Sportswear. The chic-est skiwear on *any* continent. Down-padded reversible jumpsuits, anoraks & vests. For people who only live twice. HOT STUFF!

*890 Cowan Road
Burlingame, CA 94010
415 697-8177*

WEST POINT APPAREL

Features the "Lifesaver" line of security outerwear—all reversible, with built-in safety feature of "Scotchlite" reflective trim. You light up my life.

*P.O. Box 66
Jamaica, New York 11418
212 846-4800*

WHITE SWAN MEDICAL UNIFORMS

Huge selection. Everything from young, upbeat jumpsuits to the more traditional dress that's flattering to any figure. Quite a maternity selection, too.

*White Swan/Puritan
PO Box 677
Yonkers, NY 10702
212 652-9250*

THE YAK WORKS

A must for nature nuts. Don't miss the "Optimum Series"—the Taj Mahal of tents! All the gadgets & gear you'll ever need to make your trekking life a breeze.

*2030 Westlake Avenue
Seattle, WA 98121
800 426-9935
206 623-0853 (WA)*

Our Team

Our grateful thanks to:

Stylists Franny Ruch, Andy Maag, and Fern Galperin; the Kay Models Agency Ltd., especially Donna and Frank, photo researcher Kate Somers; Terri Gleason at Capezio's, Mr. Rubin at Antler Uniform, Sarah Lee at I. Buss Hudson's, OK Uniform, the Kauffman brothers at Kauffman Saddlery; and our production staff: Larry Burns, Gordon Harris, Joan Marino, and Tony Williams.

391.04 SUA 61376
Suares, J.C.
Real clothes

OVERSIZE